PRAISE

"*The Spitboy Rule* is a compelling and insightful journey into the world of '90s punk as seen through the eyes of a Xicana drummer who goes by the nickname Todd. Todd stirs the pot by insisting that she plays hardcore punk, not riot grrrl music, and inviting males to share the dance floor with women in a respectful way. This drummer never misses a beat. Read it!"

—Alice Bag, singer for the Bags and author of *Violence Girl: East L.A. Rage to Hollywood Stage, a Chicana Punk Story*

"Incisive and inspiring, Michelle Cruz Gonzales's *The Spitboy Rule* brings the '90s punk world to life with equal parts heart and realism. Her story becomes a voyage of self-discovery, and Gonzales is the perfect guide as she writes in rapid-fire drum beats about epic road tours, female camaraderie, sexist fans, and getting accused of appropriating her own culture."

—Ariel Gore, *Hip Mama*

"Best punk memoir that I've ever had the privilege of reading. In a punk scene dominated by middle-class, white males, you can't forget Spitboy, four brave women playing music with the intensity of an out-of-control forest fire. Gonzales's involvement and presence in the punk scene, in particular, was significant because she represented a radical, feminist person of color, and she reflected a positive change in the scene for the Bay Area. Her memoir, chronicling her unique experience and perspective, occupies an important moment in the punk saga. This is a must-read for anyone still dedicated to social justice and change."

—Wendy-O Matik, author of *Redefining Our Relationships: Guidelines for Responsible Open Relationships*

"Michelle Gonzales's punk rock account is inspiring on many levels. For outsider artists, women musicians, or anybody who has ever felt the desire to forge an identity in uncharted territory, this book is detailed, heartfelt, and historically important. Briskly told in clean, conversational prose, *The Spitboy Rule* is an entertaining read and functions as an important historical, critical, and sociopolitical document of pre-internet DIY music."

—Jesse Michaels, vocalist for Operation Ivy and author of *Whispering Bodies*

The Spitboy Rule

Tales of a Xicana in a
Female Punk Band

The Spitboy Rule

Tales of a Xicana in a Female Punk Band

Michelle Cruz Gonzales

Preface by Mimi Thi Nguyen
Foreword by Martín Sorrondeguy

PMPRESS

The Spitboy Rule: Tales of a Xicana in a Female Punk Band
Michelle Cruz Gonzales © 2016
This edition published in 2016 by PM Press

ISBN: 978-1-62963-140-0
Library of Congress Control Number: 2016930958

Cover: John Yates/Stealworks.com
Cover photo: Karoline Collins
Layout: Jonathan Rowland

PM Press
P.O. Box 23912
Oakland, CA 94623

10 9 8 7 6 5 4 3 2 1

Printed in the USA by the Employee Owners of Thomson-Shore in Dexter,
Michigan
www.thomsonshore.com

Contents

The prologue introduces my character and tells the story of how someone like me, a Xicana growing up in a small town would get involved in punk rock. It addresses how and I why I was attracted to punk, the music and the politics, and how being in a band gave me a sense of identity but not a complete identity, as I was the only person of color in the band and not at all middle-class.

The opening chapter immediately sets Spitboy apart from the riot grrrl movement, one of the most controversial things about the band. It explains how we dealt with the "riot grrrl" label, how we didn't want to disrespect the movement, but also how and why we wanted to distance ourselves from it. I also admit in the piece that we may not have gone about it in the right way.

This piece details how we thoughtfully and collaboratively made the decision for the cover of our self-titled EP and why we decided not to use a photo of some graffiti that said "kill white bitch."

The strange sort of shaming people in the East Bay punk scene did to others regarding where they grew up exacerbated my insecurities about appearing too provincial, having grown up in a small town and on welfare, a fact that I did not hide but did not broadcast either. The piece introduces the sharp class differences between me and the rest of the Spitboy, a difference that would matter a lot more than we all thought.

To Sue Ann Carny and Nicole Lopez—gonna hit the town; we'll burn it down to a cinder

And for Luis Manuel, my one and only

Perhaps one did not want to be loved so much as to be understood.
—George Orwell

Preface
Mimi Thi Nguyen

S pitboy formed in 1990, the year I discovered punk and its promise to fuck shit up. I was an awkward teenager from the outer suburbs of San Diego, angry and alienated because I felt too much the omnipresence of military arrogance (especially poisonous when the first Gulf War erupted in 1991), the undocumented labor of manicured lawns and cloned housing developments, and the cruel lie of state protection (the murder of a young woman by a highway patrol officer haunted Mercy Road, less than a mile from my house). No wonder the romantic pinups of my adolescent dreaming were leather-jacketed punks throwing bricks at bank windows to protest the war or the verdict—Persian Gulf and Rodney King, respectively—and gathering in electric bursts of noise and movement. Of course, I had to move to Berkeley.

Black-clad and head-shorn (the uniform, which of course I adopted), I was told upon arrival I had to see Spitboy; an all-women anarchist feminist band was still a rarity, even in the punk capital of the Bay Area. What I remember most about their shows twenty years later are impressionistic flashes of unbound energies—like frontwoman Adrienne's warm but indomitable presence, growling as the black lace and charms tied in her hair bounced out of time with Todd's hard-hitting drumming, raging just behind her.

Because *The Spitboy Rule* conjures a particular time and place for me, I can't help but read it through that parallel view. In personal stories that resonate with familiar histories, Michelle describes her emergent consciousness during a moment that saw seismic shifts in punk, the mainstream appetite for its outsider status, and the impact of riot grrrl both on the basement stage as a space and on a national stage as a contentious crusade. (I too remember the 1993 Fugazi show Spitboy was invited to play at Fort Mason Center, and the changes it augured for the years to come. Because the anarchic record store collective where I volunteered, Epicenter Zone, sold the only available tickets, we were forced to tell—some of us more tenderly than others—so many fresh-faced youths raised on Green Day radio play that no, we did not take credit cards.) But Michelle also captures her experience of being a woman of color in punk, negotiating the idealism and cynicism of that moment in their measures.

"A BAND IS NOT AN IDENTITY."

The Spitboy Rule is Michelle's memoir, but it is also our history. For a brief moment in the early 1990s, I believed that we belonged to a chosen order—we were all punks, we shared *something* dense and bright and marvelous between us, no matter how fucked up each of us might be alone. Of course, I soon learned otherwise. The recognition that *we are not all punks the same* is also found here, in the sometimes surprising, sometimes achingly commonplace contact points between punk creed and social norm.

Oscillating between inhabiting then-Todd and now-Michelle, *The Spitboy Rule* tells stories about growing up on welfare in a boarded-up small town in inland California; about the often unarticulated distribution of punk points according to existing social hierarchies of gender, but also race and wealth, geography and knowledge (the cultural capital, for instance, of being able to properly cite source material about the Nicaraguan rebels for whom the fourth Clash album is named); and about the politics of punk names, such as when Michelle Cruz Gonzales became Todd Spitboy, claiming what we do over where we come from but, in doing so, also erasing tangled histories of migration and marginalization.

Reading these collected pieces, I was reminded of what I also fought as a young woman of color in the same scene—where racist cool provided camouflage for the same-old discourse of white supremacy in flimsy disguise; where racism (when discussed at all) was understood as something that the state or neo-Nazis committed, rather than something that was also with us; and where antiracism too often meant colorblindness. I recall too what it felt like to be at times assumed to be a "safe" brown one whose brownness goes unremarked (which Michelle describes with bracing candor), and then named the unsafe one who refuses to merely pass as "just" another punk. And I remember my own patchwork attempts to navigate how to be all parts of me at once, as Michelle did as both Xicana and punk—shorn hair and thick black winged eyeliner, Linda Ronstadt and the Subhumans on the same turntable—sometimes stumbling but always ferocious.

"WE'RE NOT A RIOT GRRRL BAND."

In the years since, histories of the era center riot grrrl to the near-eclipse of other earlier and contemporaneous punk feminisms, even though Spitboy (among other non–riot grrrl bands at the time) staunchly championed a feminist politics as well. As Michelle relates, "the band that I was now in with Karin, and Paula, and Adrienne . . . would soon be named after a female-body-centric creation story, a story that didn't involve god, a rib, or a man." What gets lost is not only the co-presence of other punk feminisms but also the valuable tensions between them.

As aggressively unapologetic women in a (still) bro-dominant scene, Spitboy shouldered both misogynist hostility and the burden of representation. How the Spitwomen did so unfolds here throughout the beats in the ordinary life of a band—selecting cover art, recording in the studio, choosing a label, touring in a crap van. Michelle tackles with honesty some of the intensely gendered questions of genre and sound (what does a punk feminist sound like?), and documents what it meant to be a woman in punk (being told to "shut up and spread your legs or play") and to be a drummer in a feminist band (as the self-dubbed "female Phil Collins of punk rock drummers"), during a historical moment when some consciousness about women in music broke through, briefly.

Alongside all the times drummer Michelle heard, "You hit hard for a girl," though, she also reflects on the cognitive dissonance of accusations directed at the Spitwomen from other feminist punks. In one of the more staggering stories, an Olympia (white) riot grrrl levied the accusation of cultural appropriation because Spitboy used Spanish to title the *Mi Cuerpo Es Mío* seven-inch. "Apparently," Michelle wryly observes, "my body is invisible." While some of the now-existing histories gesture toward the racial and class geographies of riot grrrl with either an embarrassed nod or fervent *never again*, these fractures were rarely reported in their disorienting details. Michelle illustrates so well how this accusation—a throwaway sting—unfolded for her so much about the lived experience of "coming out" as Xicana in subculture, struggling to be brown and punk at once.

It is perhaps obvious to say that *The Spitboy Rule* is crucial to our necessary (and necessarily imperfect) histories of black and brown punk, both as a reckoning with the historical politics of race and gender in punk cultures and as a genealogy that demonstrates how the past resonates in the present.

But though this book is our history, it is also Michelle's memoir. There are other stories here that paint a kaleidoscopic picture of a brown punk life, strewn with lanky boyfriends and lyric sheets, untoward assumptions of intimacy (the story about the fanboy who wants hugs, ugh) and tea and crumpets with Citizen Fish, alongside illicit border-crossings and impromptu visits to grandmothers in the city with the second largest Mexican population in the world.

In the era recounted in *The Spitboy Rule*, I remember regarding Michelle (though just a little older than me, she was a whole generation apart in punk years) as so much more worldly-wise. I have never told her this, but her glowering, glamorous presence was an inspiration to me then. As we continue to add to our punk pantheon of fierce and foundational black and brown women, she is an icon for all of us now.

MIMI THI NGUYEN is associate professor of gender and women's studies and Asian American studies at the University of Illinois, Urbana-Champaign. She is the author of *The Gift of Freedom: War, Debt, and Other Refugee Passages* (Duke University Press, 2012) and has also published in *Signs, Camera Obscura, Women & Performance, positions,* and *Radical History Review.* Nguyen has made zines since 1991, including *Slander* and *Race Riot.* She is a former *Punk Planet* columnist and *Maximumrocknroll* volunteer. She toured with other zine makers of color in 2012 and 2013, and continues to organize events and shows with and for POC punks.

Foreword
Martín Sorrondeguy

I n underground music, and in particular the punk scene, there were
so many styles and sounds to hear when the 1990s arrived, so
much exploration of music and art and ideas following in a lineage of
what came before it. Even with few resources, random scores of tapes
or records became available cheaply at the cool record shop in town or
touring band's distro box. One of the most impacting forms of learning
about a band was seeing punks decked out in the logo of a band they
loved. We would see this on jackets, patches, or T-shirts, and some
logos had so much visibility that they imprinted on our fanatical and
curious minds, leaving us wanting to hear what everyone else was "in
on." Spitboy was one of these names we all began to see everywhere.
Their logo and name began to seep into the minds of punks across the
nation.

Thinking about Spitboy and other punk women, I realized long ago
that there have always been powerful women in my life. The foundation
of which I built many of my ideas, rooted in what was handed to me
by my mother. Growing up in Chicago, I recall there being tough girls
that I had a profound admiration for—girls who took zero shit from
anyone. As I came into punk, frequenting shows at the Metro or going
to Wax Trax Records on a Saturday to shop, I recall punk women really
standing out from the crowd. One rainy evening there were two girls
decked out in leather boots and jackets, one totally bald, the other with
a black mohawk and hair dye dripping down the sides of her head. They
seemed so big to me. I was seventeen at the time and still a young timid
kid, which made them seem even bigger than they probably were. They

looked so fucking cool and I remember thinking, I want to hang out with girls like that.

In the early to mid-1990s my band Los Crudos began touring around the U.S. One of our stops, of course, was the Bay Area, which had become a massive hub for punks fleeing their small towns and the small minds of America. One vivid memory of that tour was playing a show with tons of punks hanging around a yard. That was when I finally got to meet a woman everyone called Todd, the drummer of Spitboy, a band whose graphic was already permanently in my brain. She invited Crudos to stay at her place, the Maxi Pad. The pad was a spot that had several punk women living in it and housed hundreds of touring punks during its existence. While staying with Todd, a.k.a. Michelle Gonzales, there were many conversations about subjects that pushed outside the boundaries of music. We dug her, her way of being and the way she saw the world. Her stories of growing up Xicana in Tuolumne resonated with us, and Crudos were down with her. We were hardcore city kids that came across varied stories of growing up Latino or Xicano in other parts of the country and we were fascinated with such stories. Todd was a motherfucking badass and her *cuentos* and *furias* sounded so familiar to us. We knew she was coming from the same *mierda* we had all lived through, only in another place.

We connected, as we did with so many on these tours, with other brown kids who had their own stories of struggle and survival, pressures to conform or assimilate, schooled not necessarily to learn the ABCs and 123s, but to bow under the gaze of the almighty institutions that pumped a filtered, inaccurate history told only by one side. We are survivors of these institutions and luckily we took a different road, one that led us to no longer doubt our worth. The path we took ceased to be one of shame or denial of who we were.

Todd is a *chingona*! She did not walk carelessly around her town without taking notes; scrawled in life's ink and engraved in her brain Michelle feverishly wrote things down. Every experience that moved her, good or bad, made its way into pages of her mind to be summoned at a later time. Her lyrics screamed into our faces while she beat on drums that smacked to attention every person that stood before the band.

Most kids thought they were going to witness just another show—well, fooled you. Spitboy was never that kind of band; after seeing them, everyone knew they were much more than that. One of their records was titled *Mi Cuerpo Es Mío*, and don't for a second think it is yours, motherfucker. Spitboy let you know it was not. Stopping a song mid-set to pull some smartass, drunken chump onto the stage so he can be public about why Spitboy got under his skin—these women were smart. Spitboy allowed these boys to make fools of their own damn selves, giving them the mic to spout off their generational, tired, dude vs. girl bullshit. Most, given the chance, could not even play the part well, the cheap-ass role handed down to men, sons of assholes who somehow ended up in our movement. What so many never truly understood was that all four women brought much more than playing instruments to the stage. Each member had stories, struggles, pain, and together they were searching for answers which brought them together as a band, so go ahead, talk your shit. Spitboy just handed you the fucking mic, now what do you have to say?

MARTÍN SORRONDEGUY was born in Montevideo, Uruguay, raised in the Pilsen neighborhood of Chicago, and has called San Francisco home for the last ten years. The core of Sorrondeguy's work is about addressing inequities through the creation of physical and artistic space—first as the singer of the internationally renowned politically charged punk en Español hardcore band Los Crudos. For the last fifteen years, Sorrondeguy has been the singer of the queercore band Limp Wrist. He recently completed his third photography book, *En busca de algo más* (Ugly Records, Buenos Aires).

Prologue: A Band Is Not an Identity

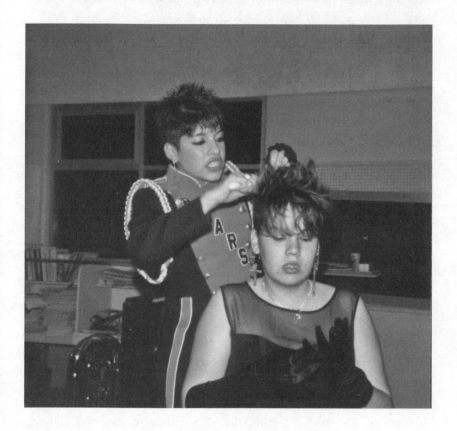

When I heard the Go-Go's for the first time, I was already in a band—the school band. I played the flute. Flute was pretty and it seemed like a good choice of instrument for a girl. I decorated the case with unicorn stickers and carried it to school every day by the slender leather handle, glad that I hadn't decided to play trombone.

When I heard the Go-Go's, that was it. I was going to be in a rock band, a female rock band. I had already spent hours and hours singing along to Joni Mitchell's *Court and Spark*, one of my favorite records in my mom's collection. I even choreographed a dance routine to the song "Twisted" to perform in a talent show with my friend Tara. My mom sewed silver rickrack on black leotards so we'd have matching outfits. The song has a line about how the narrator's analyst tells her she's crazy and she tells him he's the one with the problem, that she's known since childhood that she was a genius. I had never heard anything like it, and I hadn't yet read "The Yellow Wallpaper." I listened to Linda Ronstadt too. Nobody really knew back then that she was Mexican American. I must have looked at the photos of her in the *Simple Dreams* album jacket hundreds of times, staring into her big brown eyes.

But the Go-Go's made it look so good. They added power in numbers and a certain defiance, women rocking out, doing this thing that men acted like you had to have dick to do. An all-female band, a women's space, that made sense to me, having been raised by women, wild women, horse women, seamstresses, baby whisperers, culinary whizzes, and expert bakers, who taught me the value of creativity in women's spaces.

Then I heard the Clash. That was it. I was going to be in a punk band, an all-female punk band that stood for something, a band that would write songs like "Twisted," songs that spoke out against the mismeasure of women. That would be even better.

I suppose I could say that I'm not sure what attracted me to punk rock, but that wouldn't be true. Punk rock: the loud, hard, angry, fast music attracts angry people; angsty teenagers; social misfits; kids whose parents are too strict, straight, Christian; kids whose parents abused them; kids who witnessed any other kind of violence in the home; seemingly normal kids who don't feel so normal on the inside. Interestingly, punk rock attracts working-class kids, kids who grew up in poverty, and kids from privileged families.

I grew up on welfare, raised by a single mom in a tiny town in the California foothills. Not too far from the Bay Area, Tuolumne County attracted all kind of hippies: psychedelic hippies, drug-addict hippies, gardening pastoral fantasy hippies, wannabe American Indian hippies, save-Mother-Earth hippies, herbal healer hippies, Grateful Dead hippies, and of course, your run-of-the-mill dirty hippies. If not for being raised by a strong woman whose influences on me, negative and positive, were profound, I could have rebelled against subculture movements. But as a Mexican American, a Xicana in a hick town, I was never allowed to forget that I didn't fit in, that I muddied their waters.

I would show them.

I started listening for the sounds of rebellion on my clock radio, the sounds of the Clash and the Go-Go's crackling their way through the single speaker. Later that year, my sister's middle-class grandparents bought me a knockoff Walkman. I recorded songs to a cassette player from the radio to absorb through the foam covered headphones, and when I had saved enough babysitting money, I bought *Prince Charming* by Adam and the Ants. Adam Ant was my third celebrity crush after Harrison Ford's Han Solo and Olivia Newton-John. I can remember baking in the sun in my hot pink swimsuit at the Tuolumne Pool and listening to "Scorpions," letting the sun sear into my skin because it matched how I felt inside listening to Adam Ant sing.

But in 1983, I went to the US Festival to see the Clash, and Joe Strummer said something that made me forget about celebrity crushes, fickle chameleons who dress in costume and change their identities with every record:

> You make, you buy, you die. That's the motto of
> America. You get born to buy, and I'll tell you those
> people out in East LA they ain't going to stay there
> forever. If there's anything going to be in the future it's
> going to be all parts of everything. It's not going to be
> just one white way down the middle of the road.

I felt he was speaking directly to me, a Mexican American from East LA, now living in a small town, bringing my version of Mexicanisma to our corner of the state. I went home straight after the three-day festival (skipping the metal day in the middle), cut my hair short, and started paying even more attention to the world around me and my place in it.

I would show them. I would show my own mother, too. She still believed that Mexican girls should keep their hair long.

I bought Aqua Net and Maybelline eyeliner in black, the kind with the pointy red cap that I watched my chola cousins in LA heat with a match before applying to their eyes, rimming the water line dark black and penciling all around the outside, too, enhancing the almond shape of their eyes with a long black wing.

Tuolumne saw a shabby Mexican girl, a freak, so I was going to give them one. But I looked good, too. I saw that the look suited me, enhanced who I really was, who my mom hoped nobody saw she might be, a Xicana from East LA, the person she covered up with the long jean skirts and macramé tops. Having much darker hair and skin than my mother, I couldn't pass. And maybe she wasn't trying to pass so much as trying to fit in somewhere where being a woman didn't have so many rules.

I wanted to fit in somewhere, too, but I also wanted to create something, so after several years of playing flute in the school band and later the high school marching band, learning marching band formations on the football field during half-time, I taught myself to play drums. A high school senior and Me-Wuk tribe member, Kevin Bernido, actually did give me a few drumming tips and my punk name, Todd, a name that would stick because I had such a crush on him that I would have answered to just about anything he wanted to call me. My best friend Nicole Lopez, who had an absent Mexican dad and a white, born and raised in Tuolumne mother, learned to play guitar, and we enlisted my other childhood friend, Suzy, to sing. After learning a couple of covers and teaching her stoner punk friend Christina to play bass, we became Bitch Fight. When we weren't in school or hanging out with the handful of other punk kids in the county, we were practicing at Nicole's house or my place, writing new songs, and preparing to graduate high school and get the hell out of there. Before moving, we kicked Chris out of the band because we felt that she cared too much about getting stoned and hanging out with her boyfriend. Nicole, Suzy, and I were serious about the band because we knew it was our ticket to making friends and a name for ourselves in San Francisco. We couldn't bear to move out of Tuolumne and become small fish. And the three of us did move, and make friends, and play several shows at Gilman in Berkeley, but we fought a lot too, not quite appreciating or knowing how to navigate the women's space, opting to get caught up in petty jealousies. Suzy and I always fought for attention, especially Nicole's. If we had a leader, Nicole was it, the young visionary in the band.

I learned a lot in Bitch Fight: how to have more patience, to listen more, to collaborate better, to put jealousy in check and my ego too.

I started again.

I sought out women with whom I could play music: women who wanted to start the band that we wanted to hear, a band that played as hard as men did, but sounded like women. And I wanted to write songs about women's issues and to get along—do what Bitch Fight did not have the maturity to do. But I gave up a lot, losing my friendships with Nicole, Suzy, and Elka (who joined the band on guitar when we moved to San Francisco) from Bitch Fight, finding my own way to fit into the Bay Area scene, and putting Tuolumne behind me. Alone, I wasn't quite prepared to understand that it wasn't just being Xicana and 1990s colorblindness that prevented me from always feeling like I never quite fit in. It was the difference in my class background (something I shared with Bitch Fight) that would also intrude, that would set me apart. It also gave me a unique perspective, a perspective that I tried to ignore for a long time, but it never let me forget it was there, gnawing at me, reminding me that being in an all-female hardcore punk band wasn't the only way to define myself.

Not a Riot Grrrl Band

"SPITBOY are the best girl band around. They piss all over every Riot Grrrl band I can think of. They've got more power in their dirty little fingernails than Courtney Love, Kathleen Hanna and Kat Bjelland put together. . . . Tonight, these four women, sweaty and angry, but also (between songs) witty and endearing—have stolen my heart. . . . Spitboy are uniquely inspiring, not only for their awesome bile, but also for their straightforwardness. They hate sexism, not men. They know exactly what they're talking about and how to articulate their righteous aggression."

—*Melody Maker*, April 10, 1993, London, England
"Live!" review by Lucy Sweet

I t happened in Washington, DC, an already strange city, which added to the day's angst. After getting lost on one-way streets and roundabouts, we found our way to the venue we were scheduled to play that day, a sort of loft space storefront on a swanky tree-lined street with Victorian architecture, a strange place to play after playing church basements and Elks Lodges in the Midwest.

I followed Adrienne out of the van, staying at the heels of her clunky boots, as I often did during times like these. Adrienne was outgoing and became even more so when in doubt. I tended toward standoffishness. We weren't playing with any riot grrrl bands that day, but members of Bikini Kill and the guys from Nation of Ulysses, who they were all hanging around with, were there for the show. Bay Area bands were a draw, and women came out when Spitboy played. Bikini Kill and their friends had come out to see us play, to see what we were all about.

Adrienne marched up to the door of the venue looking for the guy who had set up the show to find out where we should load in. I figured I could get past the intimidating moments of meeting new people and unfamiliar scenesters faster if I hung with Adrienne while she went around, smiling her straight-toothed wide smile, her blue eyes sparkling, introducing herself to people, laughing easily, shaking people's hands, and hugging those who wanted a hug. I stopped at shaking hands. I didn't want people I didn't know hugging me or touching me, men in particular, no matter how much they liked Spitboy, and not when I was already feeling tense about being on riot grrrl territory.

Like the label "riot grrrl," hugs had become a sore subject. Earlier in the tour, on our way out of some city, this guy, a friend of our tour contact, had offered to give us all hugs. Apparently, I was the only one in the band who found this creepy. "Everyone tells me I give the best hugs. Do you want a hug?" the young man said, holding his arms out, waiting for one of us to step in. He was a pale-faced, chubby dude, not fat, just a little husky, the kind of punk guy who was probably vegetarian but who rarely ate vegetables and subsisted on mainly cheese and bread and beer or soda.

"Sure, I'll have a hug." Adrienne smiled wide and stepped forward.

I took a step back and looked toward our dented blue van.

"You do give the best hugs." Adrienne turned to Karin who was standing at her side. "Karin, you have to get one of his hugs."

Karin stepped forward and let this guy hug her, hugging him back.

I could see the guy's face as he hugged Karin, his head over her shoulder, his eyes scrunching with the squeeze of his arms, his goofy smile.

"Okay, I'll have one too," Paula said.

I stepped to the side to avoid his line of vision once he opened his eyes.

"Thank you," Paula said, once he released her. She smiled a real smile, her freckles dancing about.

I looked down at the ground, to where the asphalt met the dirt on the side of the road. I could feel all eyes on me.

"Do you want a hug too?" Huggy Bear Boy smiled and stepped in my direction.

"No, I don't," I said before he got too close. "Thank you," I added.

Huggy Bear Boy stopped his forward lumber, and there was an awkward silence as he lowered his arms, like two long animal balloons out of air.

In the van, I felt like I had to explain myself, as if the band's motto "my body is mine" didn't extend to contact with fans.

"But he was nice," Adrienne said.

Karin and Paula were in the front seat waving at Huggy Bear Boy and his friend as we drove away. I waved and forced a smile because I didn't want to look like a total asshole.

"That was probably the most action that guy's gotten in days, maybe ever," I said once we had driven a block or so.

"Todd," Karin said, shocked, but she laughed anyway because she knew it was probably true.

Even though I didn't want to be hugged by fans unless I felt some kind of real connection, like after a conversation, I was oddly confident in other ways. I didn't usually get nervous before playing live, but I was nervous the night we played in front of members of Bikini Kill and

Nation of Ulysses. I felt intimidated. Then a tall guy came up to me before we played to ask if we required the men in the crowd to stand in the back of the room, like they were told to do during a Bikini Kill set. I couldn't believe my ears, but I now had someplace to direct my angst.

At my drum set, I pulled my vocal mic up to my mouth, "Before we play, we'd just like to say that we don't expect men to stand in the back of the room. We're not a riot grrrl band." All the air sucked right out of the room as soon as I said it. Mouths dropped open and silent. It was as if someone had turned off the sound.

Being the hot-headed one, I had nominated myself to say something about what we realized had become an elephant in the room, but I had chosen my words poorly, spoke too soon, shat where I ate. I had blasphemed in the sacred church of riot grrrl, broken the trance. But there it was, out in the open: we were a female punk band in 1992, but we were not a riot grrrl band. It was probably best for the rest of the band that I had been the one to say it, as I was the one who would became the most hated Spitwoman of just about every riot grrrl thereafter, because I was the scrappy one, the only one who didn't grow up middle-class, the only nonwhite one; I had grown thicker skin and a chip on my shoulder. But they backed me up; Spitboy was great this way. We did sometimes discuss possible approaches and reactions to familiar crowd responses, but we never shut down anyone in the band who felt passionate about something, and when one of us spoke first on a topic, there was always room for another of us to chime in and add her two cents. In this case, Adrienne stepped into recover some sense of decorum.

"Please don't block a woman's view; don't stand in front of someone who is shorter than you are. Just use common sense."

I appreciated Adrienne's attempt to soften the blow of my comment, but my hands and knees had started to shake and wouldn't stop the second the words, "We're not a riot grrrl band" were out there and I saw the stunned looks on people's faces. But we weren't trying to piss on riot grrrl. It would have been easier to say we were a riot grrrl band because we stood for most of the same things, except there were three important distinctions: we had formed Spitboy in the Bay Area during the early days of their movement, we didn't endorse separatism, and we didn't want to be called girls.

This one public comment, saying aloud what we had discussed with one another only privately until then, forever altered our relationship with one of the most influential women's movements in the punk rock scene nationwide and created an uneasy rivalry. Still, we had discussed it and had made the deliberate decision not to send boys to the back. It was true, we hated sexism; we didn't hate men, and neither did Bikini Kill. If we could go back and do it over again, though, we might have done it differently. Maybe I would have gone about it less bluntly, or somehow differently. But not much, not much differently.

Kill White Bitch

When it came time for Spitboy to release its first seven-inch record, Paula, Karin, Adrienne, and I had a lot of decisions to make. Deciding which songs would make the record was actually easy, as we didn't have many songs to begin with. Somehow, the task didn't intimidate us, even though I was the only one who had ever been in a band who had put out a record. Karin and Paula had been volunteering at Blacklist Mailorder in San Francisco, and Adrienne had experience with laying out art, having done her zine for a couple of years already. After coming up with the name—which writer and later singer of Gag Order, Wendy O'Matik, helped us do—our first big decision as a band was what we'd put on the cover of the first record. It would mark how we worked collaboratively over the next six years, discussing our goals, generating ideas, sharing them without ego, trying things out, and making real group decisions.

These discussions usually took place in our practice space in East Oakland near Laney College. Before practice or between songs, we'd stand around and discuss what kind of artwork we wanted to represent us. I'd be sitting behind my drum set, and Karin and Paula would still be wearing their guitars. It took quite a bit of discussion to have any sense of what kind of image or graphic we could use to represent us, a female punk band that sang about women's issues, but we gravitated toward photographs. During one of these evening-after-work-all-day practice sessions, Adrienne told us about some graffiti that she passed by every day on her way to work. She worked on Telegraph Avenue, and even though she had a car she walked the two or so miles there to avoid having to pay for parking and to stay in shape. In fact, Adrienne rarely drove. Being a bit nervous behind the wheel, she preferred to walk whenever she could. She walked to work, the store, the mailbox, her boyfriend's house, and wherever else she could when it wasn't dangerous for her to do so. I had experienced a great deal of harassment on the streets, so now that I had a car, I avoided walking, even short distances. It was this experience of being harassed on the streets, something we talked a great deal about, a subject of one of our songs, "The Threat," that caused Adrienne to notice the crudely scribbled phrase on the wall of the Highway 24 overpass on the Oakland side of Telegraph Avenue on her way to work. It said "kill white bitch."

"I'm going to bring my camera tomorrow and take a picture," Adrienne said. "I'll get the film developed over the weekend and bring the pictures to practice on Monday."

We all agreed that taking a picture of the offending graffiti and bringing the pictures to practice for us all to see was a good idea, a good place to start in our search for cover art.

On Monday, Adrienne pulled the photos out of her backpack. She had taken several, and she passed them out for us to look at. I cringed when I saw the graffiti. It was not large, but it was there among other crude scribbles and green ivy that crawled up the wall of the overpass. It had very little artistic merit, but it did make a statement.

"I don't know," I said, unable to even figure out why I didn't feel good about what I saw and why I didn't think it would make a good cover for our first record.

"Hmmm . . ." Karin said.

"It does show the kind of danger women are in," Adrienne said.

"It does do that," Karin said.

"Yeah, it does," I said, "but what would we be saying about the person who wrote it?"

I also wanted to say something about how the term "white bitch" didn't apply to me, but I didn't quite know how to articulate this point, as I didn't often make references to being Mexican, a Xicana, in a mostly white band in a mostly white punk scene. It was just easier to try to blend in with my short hair, my tattoo, and my punk uniform.

Paula, who was savvier this way, having a more natural understanding of issues facing marginalized groups than the rest of us (I had lived these issues but had not yet learned to analyze my own life) finally spoke up.

"If we use a photo of this graffiti, we'd be making a statement about race more than women's safety on the streets. We'd be accusing the person who wrote it of being both a misogynist and a racist, and I don't think we're trying to do that, even if it was true."

We all nodded because what Paula said made a lot of sense.

"I didn't think about it that way," Adrienne said, "but you're right."

"And I'm not white, so it doesn't really apply to all of us," I said, finally finding some words to cover how I felt.

To that I got no response, but at least I had gotten it out.

Because we didn't want to confuse our message, we went with a different photo, but this is how we worked, through thoughtful discussion and by consensus, which is how we made our final decision. The self-titled Spitboy seven-inch features a blurry black-and-white nude of Adrienne, her arms captured in motion in front of her, the background behind her a dark, dark black. It was a photo taken by a photographer friend, a session done in the spirit of Adrienne embracing her new leaner body with all its beautiful curves, and it embodied a powerful positive spirit, a fierce femaleness, but away from the victim-focused negativity of our original idea.

Punk Points

In the 1990s, before we understood race and class privilege, we just thought it wasn't cool if you grew up in the suburbs. It wasn't cool to be from Walnut Creek, Concord, or Fremont, but a lot of punk kids who hung around the East Bay Gilman scene grew up in those cities. It wasn't cool to be from Walnut Creek because that meant you came from money, and it wasn't cool to be from Fremont because that was total suburbia. But of course not everyone could be from Berkeley, Oakland, or San Francisco.

It wasn't cool, especially in my mind, to be from a small town either. Small towns were too quaint, not gritty enough, too provincial. The only person who thought it was cool that I was from a small town, from Tuolumne, was Aaron Elliott of Crimpshrine. He even thought it was cool after I took him there one summer. I worried that after taking him to Tuolumne that he'd think otherwise, but he didn't. I have a photograph of him on a rock at the Clavey River in cut-off jean shorts, his bleached blond hair aglow among the flinty black-and-white granite rock.

Aaron was also the rare guy who thought it was cool to date a girl drummer, someone like him, but not, all at the same time. I was taken with his long-armed, pointy-kneed, awkward drumming style, full lips, and bleach blond hair, and I let him pursue me until I was ready to break up with the mysterious, oft-distant, stagehand boyfriend who said he was Italian, even though his mom and sister looked distinctly Mexican. Aaron liked my brown skin, and he liked talking about the fact that I was from a small town. He told me that that Bitch Fight should stop saying we were from San Francisco and say we were from Tuolumne instead. He had a way of seeing things that many of us at that age could not, even if he got a little bossy about it. Still, I liked that he wanted to get to know where I was from and how he could both define and subvert the punk points system all at the same time. But he couldn't understand why I didn't want to be from Tuolumne. I couldn't explain it because I didn't understand it either.

After bringing it up a number of times, he brought it up again at the apartment at Haight and Webster that I shared with Nicole. It was late morning. He had spent the night, and the sun was shining bright through the wide Victorian window. We were getting ready to make our way back to the East Bay, probably for some punk show.

"It would be way cooler if you said you were from Tuolumne. No other bands are from Tuolumne."

The bright light from the window suddenly hurt my eyes.

"But we're not. Elka's not."

I tried not to whine. I wanted to explain myself better, to find words, but I couldn't. At eighteen, I didn't have the maturity or courage to match up against the swirl of feelings inside, the guilt over leaving my brother and sister with my drug-addicted mother, the shame of growing up shabby and on welfare, the anger about being treated like a minority, othered.

Trapped by the anger, I could say that Aaron was different too: nerdy, awkward, and punk rock, and that the punk rock part was just an attitude, all ripped jeans, and weird shit tied to his wrists, things he could take off. But I know it's a little more complicated than that; it always is.

Even though neither the suburbs nor a small town got you punk points, being from a small town like Tuolumne was the opposite of being from a place like Walnut Creek. Tuolumne wasn't a quaint place like some people thought it was. Twain Harte, the resort town up the hill, that was quaint. Even Sonora, the county seat, could be considered quaint, but not Tuolumne. Tuolumne was run-down. The majority of the storefronts in the block known as downtown were boarded up the majority of the time; only the bars managed to stay in business. The building next door to the Youth Center off Main Street had a restaurant kitchen, but a restaurant never managed to stay open there for more than a year, because anyone who could afford to eat out preferred to drive to Sonora or Twain Harte to do that. There were a few people in town who had a little money, but most lived month to month, or in our case from food stamp to food stamp. Until the age of twelve, we didn't even have a TV in the house. For many years, my mom did not believe in television, an idea she learned from her Bay Area hippie friends. It was convenient not to believe in something that she couldn't afford. The first TV we had in our house belonged to her first serious boyfriend after she separated from my sister's father.

Even before the punk points system, I was influenced by my own set of standards, and for somebody who had become interested in politics and social issues, not having a TV was actually quite a detriment. Nicole's mom made us watch the news with her. She thought it was important for us to keep up on unrest in Nicaragua and El Salvador, only I could never follow what was going on. My mom is a smart woman, but she didn't read much, and she got kicked out of high school in eleventh grade when they found out that she was pregnant with me. I remember her sitting around the front room with a joint, reading the *Lord of the Rings* books and books about Merlin, which she tried to get me to read, but she didn't read the newspaper or follow any particular issues. She obviously preferred fantasy to reality.

Watching the national evening news at Nicole's house made me question my intelligence. It was a good thing that Nicole's mom was so invested in knowing as much as she could about US involvement in Central America, because she would summarize the news reports for us, and even record them on a cassette player so we could listen back to them later.

After Nicole and her mom would drop me off at home after an evening of watching the news and doing some homework, I'd walk up my long dirt driveway and wonder why, even when I concentrated really hard, I couldn't follow what was going on. Wasn't the news supposed to be for everybody?

Somewhere along the way, long before being in Spitboy, I had internalized a deep desire to be smart. Nicole and her mom were super smart and that impressed me, and growing up in the 1970s and '80s, a time when someone like me did not fit the beauty standard, I wasn't tempted to try to get by in the world on my looks, but it wasn't just that. The women who raised me, my mom and her friends, knew a little about everything and some were specialists. My aunt Jude was an expert on horses, my mother was an expert seamstress, and my aunt Kathy was the baby whisperer. Until Nicole, her mom, and I joined the Sonora antiwar group, I didn't know any other people besides Nicole's mom who cared about international affairs. Being interested in politics and not being able to understand the news bothered me. I wanted to be an expert, too. No one I knew spoke the way they did on the news, so serious and formal and buttoned up, interjecting assertions with sound bites, cutting away to interviews. I thought I was just too stupid to understand.

When Nicole, Suzy, and I got to San Francisco in 1987, everyone seemed so much more sophisticated, so much more punk. We weren't hicks, but we had grown up in a hick town and we didn't want it to show. We took constant mental notes on how shit was done in the Bay Area and how to act at shows. Suzy wore more eyeliner, Nicole dressed even more like a skater, I stopped using so much Aqua Net, and we all started crimping our hair. We told people where we lived too, any chance we got.

"We live on Delmar Street, just off Haight," one of us would say when asked.

"Just up the street from Rasputin's." I thought it was super cool to live up the street from an actual record store.

We wanted to belong and to prove we weren't country bumpkins. I wanted people to think that I had always understood that the Clash's *Sandinista* album was named after the Nicaraguan rebels, headed by Daniel Ortega, who overthrew years and years of dictatorial rule under the Somoza family, that the nightly national news only told part of the story, and that Ronald Reagan funded the death squads in El Salvador.

Of course, like Bitch Fight, none of Spitboy was originally from Berkeley, Oakland, or San Francisco, the cities where we lived, but I was the only member who grew up in a small town, who was raised by a single mom, and who had been raised in relative poverty. In Spitboy, I didn't have to work hard to appear edgy and gritty at all. I had a lot of punk rock cred because I had been in two bands already, but in Spitboy I felt I had to work hard to appear smart, knowledgeable about the issues, not one in particular, but all of them, and not let it show that I was once someone who couldn't understand TV news or had a drug-addicted mom. Born into relative comfort and white privilege Karin, Paula, and Adrienne's identities may have been easier to navigate, but if they weren't careful, they could lose punk points too.

Paula who grew up in San Jose and had lived for a bit in San Diego, and who was living in a warehouse in Oakland when I met her, was seemingly the most worldly, but Karin was from the Midwest, and Adrienne was from Pleasanton. Pleasanton, California, the wealthiest of the tri-valley cities, just over the hill from Oakland, the city with some of the best schools in California, is one of the least punk rock cities in the state, mainly just for its name: Pleasanton. Adrienne wouldn't really ever evade the question of where she grew up, but she didn't trumpet it from the hilltops either. She would actually laugh, embarrassed, when she said it because saying that she was from a place called Pleasanton wasn't punk at all.

Karin on the other hand didn't seem to have any hangups about where she was from and, really, there's no reason that she should have. None of us gets to choose our background. Karin, who moved to San Francisco from Missouri, was actually born in Germany where they lived for her father's job at Boeing. Her parents, very kind people who went on sailing vacations in the British Virgin Islands and served good wine with dinner, supported Karin's decisions to move to the Bay Area and join a punk band, and they took an interest in the band and what we were about. They seemed to really believe that their daughter, who had earned BAs in French and journalism before leaving the Midwest, was prepared to make her own decisions and was well enough educated to provide for herself. Admittedly, I never understood the sailing, but I admired what the Gembus family had been able to do for their children—educate them, love them, believe in them, and let them be.

But it wasn't lost on me that I was the only person in the band raised by a single mom, the only one who didn't have still-married parents who went on real vacations. I was determined not to feel less of myself as a result. Still, none of the Spitwomen ever went to Tuolumne, never saw the rickety house that I grew up in, or swam in the Clavey River, met my wild mother, or had a real sense of how I grew up other than from what came out here and there. I never thought to invite them to Tuolumne, because the longer I was away the more I began seeing the world through their eyes.

Without them, I already knew that Tuolumne was dysfunctional, limiting, broken, but I was not.

Flowers of Evil

I found the artwork used on the Spitboy logo while looking through Damon Douglass's books. Damon was a transplant from New York, lured to the Bay Area by the thriving punk scene. *Flowers of Evil*, where I found the artwork, was sitting atop a stack of books in an old milk crate in the loft living room, just off the kitchen in the warehouse rented by Damon and my then boyfriend Neil Grimmer, a sculpture artist who'd later form the short-lived but impactful Paxston Quiggly.

The striking blocky image of a nude woman with one arm across her face took my breath away. I had woken early and gone up to the kitchen to make some coffee, grabbed the book, and sat down on the sagging, dingy couch to read a bit while I waited for my coffee to brew. The light from the skylight filtering over the couch was just right for reading, and I intended to read a couple of the Baudelaire poems in the *Flowers of Evil* collection when I saw the first illustration. When I saw it, I stopped caring about trying to understand Baudelaire. I turned each page with text quickly away until I found the next image. Published by Peter Pauper Press out of New York, this edition of *Flowers of Evil* was illustrated with woodcut nudes of women. All the images commanded your attention with their heavy black lines. Some depicted love scenes, but the majority of them were of women alone, striking and naked. The second I saw the woodcut of the woman, nude with her hand across her face, I knew I had found the Spitboy logo. The image was intensely female, strong, and vulnerable too, like us.

The woodcut itself, with its heavy black lines depicts a woman with large clenched hand covering her eyes. The hand over her face implies some type of anguish, but without shame, for she's simultaneously nude, open, baring her breast. A large dark pink nipple draws the viewer's eye to the center of the woodcut. The heavy dark lines of the woman's hair are striking too, hanging down in sharp points pointing toward her navel in the center of her ample belly. The original heavy-lined woodcut has a pink background, but since we did not have access to color copying, I knew the version we'd use would come out in black and white, which was also more punk rock.

The font used for the title of the book *Flowers of Evil* is unusual, a heavy, dark font with pointy serifs, and I happened to find something similar in some art materials lying around the warehouse, a sheet of scratch on letters, the kind used to make signs or small posters before widespread access to computers. There were several different sheets of lettering, and one of them happened to be in the same style of the font in the book. I took the book and the letters to Krishna Copy Center in Berkeley, made a photo copy of the image, and used the scratch-on lettering to spell Spitboy, creating what is now known as the Spitboy logo, not at all knowing, or hoping, or having any idea that it would become the image that would live on to define and represent us for so long.

When I found the images in *Flowers of Evil*, Spitboy hadn't been together long. We were planning to play our first show in the 42nd Street warehouse, the very same warehouse where I found the book, and we had discussed making a sheet with our lyrics on it to pass out to anyone in the crowd who might be interested in what we had to say. We had, however, been more focused on writing songs and practicing than thinking much about things like lyric sheets or logos. Artwork wasn't something that we were naturally inclined to. Many people in the scene, like Neil Grimmer, found or borrowed images and made stencils, something Neil was good at already. He did this for Econochrist and later for Paxston Quiggly. It wasn't uncommon for punk bands to lift or borrow something found in a magazine or a book and use it as an image for an album or as a logo, and it was important for us to find just the right thing since none of us in Spitboy had Neil's talents. What we did have was a good eye for striking images, and all the Spitwomen agreed that Jeff Hill's woodcut from *Flowers of Evil* would make a great logo or at least look good on a couple of lyric sheets.

It felt good at that first show to have lyric sheets and a logo. We played mostly for our friends that day, so it was an offering of sorts, a way to help them see us in this new way. Members of Filth, Neurosis, and Econochrist were in the audience. I could feel every person in the warehouse with its cement floors, high ceilings, and skylights focused on our femaleness, focused on the fact that we were women about to play what everyone thought of as male music. Sitting behind my drum set before the first song, looking out onto the crowd, I realized that the show was a test of sorts too, a can they pull this off? I had been excited to share Spitboy with our community for the first time, now I wasn't sure looking out onto what had become a blur of hard unfamiliar faces. We got nods of approval when our set was over, but the men in the scene somehow made it clear that we would not get the same respect that they gave each other. We were still a novelty and a challenging one at that.

Spitboy had seen a couple of other bands pass out lyric sheets, but it wasn't a common practice. We later decided to pass out lyric sheets for every show, a practice that we continued overseas, even paying to have our lyrics translated into Spanish, German, and Italian. I loved seeing women at our shows at the front of the stage scanning the lyric sheet for the next song, nodding their heads and smiling as they read. In the end, reaching them and seeing their approval was what mattered most.

The Threat

S pitboy recorded our first self-titled record with Kevin Army, a really great guy who would serve as both our engineer and guide. Spitboy had at that point only recorded one song, "Seriously," a straightforward three- or four-chord punk rock song with Adrienne singing lead vocals and me singing backup just a bit behind her in the style that we had picked up somewhere along the way. It wasn't until we were in the studio with Kevin that we discovered something terrible—recorded singing backup all together, we sounded like screeching females.

We had spent a day recording the songs, leaving the vocals for last, as has to be done in the studio. Having had what can only be described as an out of body experience recording my vocals for "Ultimate Violations," a song I wrote about sexual assault and the afteraffects it has on women,

I felt in very good hands with Kevin. He didn't seem at all fazed that I stopped between each take to shed a different item of clothing, first my shoes, then my socks, then the top I had been wearing over a tank top, probably some band T-shirt. He listened, looking concerned, when I described the sensation of floating up in the corner of the room viewing myself from above during the good take, exorcising my own painful experience with assault.

Once Adrienne had recorded her vocals for the song "The Threat," a song she wrote about what it's like to walk the streets at night as a woman, the fear we felt and the injustice of it, the rest of us, Paula, Karin, and I now had to record our vocals. All we had to do was to sing what we sang live. But when Kevin played it back for us to hear, watching for our reaction from behind the glass in the engineer's booth, the three of us looked frantically back and forth among one another. We had developed a hardcore sound that we liked, the sound that we had wanted to hear women play, but we found ourselves faced with a terrible dilemma. We wanted to sound like women, but we didn't want to sound like *that*.

One of us signaled for Kevin to stop the track, "Is that what we sound like?"

"We sound so screechy."

"So high-pitched."

"Is that really what we sound like?" one of us asked again.

I could see Kevin reach over and press the button to turn on his mic.

"Yes, that's what you sound like." He smiled his trademark wide smile.

"We don't want to sound like that," one of us said into her mic.

"You don't want to sound how you sound?"

"Not like that."

We were all speaking into our shared microphone, taking turns trying to express how we felt, our headphones still on so we could hear Kevin through the glass.

"It's just that we sound so screechy."

It seemed like a terrible contradiction. We wanted to sound like women, but we didn't want to screech, we didn't want to grate, and we knew of course that stereotypes about women were influencing how we felt, as Kevin had tried to gently point out. Still, we knew we had to rerecord the track, so we asked Kevin to let us start again.

"We'd like to do another take," Karin said into the mic.

And without discussing it or planning, each of us knew what she had to do, lower her voice a register or two and deliver backing vocals that didn't sound like Edith Bunker from *All in the Family*.

"Threatening, threatening, threatening!"

And even though I always felt a little bad about it, I know I sang my vocals in that same lower register whenever we played that song live thereafter.

The Female Phil Collins of Punk Rock Drummers

When I first started playing drums, I had no idea that there were so many stereotypes about drummers, nor did I realize what a spectacle I'd become—a woman playing drums! Of course I did know that singers in a band get all the attention and that everyone thinks that guitar players are cool, but somehow I didn't know that drummers are often depicted as blockheaded dolts, only good for keeping a beat and just about nothing else. None of the drummers I knew growing up fit this stereotype, and being a female drummer, I would have never thought that it applied to me.

Spitboy was in England with Citizen Fish when I first became aware of the dumb-drummer stereotypes. Trotsky and I were loading the drums into some venue on a gray afternoon before the soundcheck. Spider, the Amebix drummer was hanging around chatting with us when he pointed out a sign on a tall metal cabinet just off the stage. It said something like, "Musicians don't block this cabinet. This means you too, drummers."

I had to read the sign a couple of times before I got the joke.

"That's terrible," I said, laughing more out of embarrassment than anything else because I didn't really think the sign was funny at all. I did think it would be amusing to have someone take our picture next to it, and I gave my camera to someone nearby to snap the shot. In the photo, Spider, Trotsky, and I are making "dumb drummer" faces and the sign is only sort of visible because that dolt Spider is partially blocking it.

* * *

I taught myself to play the drums when I was fifteen, after failing to learn to play guitar. My friends Nicole and Suzy and I wanted to start a band. We made up names for the band before learned to play our instruments, and it's a good thing that it took us a while to learn to play because that gave us the time to realize that we should be named Bitch Fight and not Combined Force or The Future. Nicole wanted to play bass, and I was supposed to play guitar, so I started taking lessons, bringing a songbook of Clash songs with me so I could learn some songs that I actually liked and not "House of the Rising Sun." I sucked at guitar, and my hippie guitar teacher, Tim, wasn't very encouraging about teaching me to play the Clash.

"These are the worst songs," he said, sitting on a chair next to me with his acoustic guitar. He wore a floppy suede hat, the kind often worn by hippies who still wished it was the 1960s or '70s. It even had a braided embellishment around the brim and a coin buckle, probably a buffalo coin.

We were in small music shop in Sonora where I took lessons. My mom had somehow hooked me up with Tim. He was the friend of one of her many hippie friends. I didn't say anything. I just looked out the glass window in the room where he gave lessons. I could see cars driving up Highway 108.

"Are you sure you wouldn't want to learn some better songs?" he groused.

"I just want to learn to play," I said.

I didn't want to start trouble, and I figured if the Clash songs were as easy as he said they were then I could learn them at home.

But the truth was that I had a hard time learning any songs. Tim taught me to play "Louie, Louie," and of course, "House of the Rising Sun," but what I really needed to learn to play punk rock were bar chords. Playing the flute all through elementary and high school hadn't been much preparation for playing bar chords, which requires a great deal of hand, finger, and joint strength and dexterity. Nicole quickly got better than me, causing us to rethink our lineup. Suzy was still going to sing because she didn't have any instrument training at all, but now Nicole would have to play guitar, and I was going to learn drums. I didn't tell anyone how relieved I was to not have to learn how to play guitar even though I had begged my mom for a guitar and amp for Christmas, and she had bought them both. Now I was going to have to ask for drums.

When I had told Mr. Wells, my music teacher, that I was going to teach myself to play drums in the music appreciation class, he told me that flute players make great drummers, though he never explained why. Somehow, I knew I'd be able to play the drums, to handle directing each limb to move in a different way on different beats all at the same time, and I was right. Within a couple of months of being in the music appreciation class, Nicole, Suzy, and I started practicing, playing covers at first, and soon after, writing our own songs.

I never had anything against the drums or drummers, hadn't been exposed to the stupid stereotypes, and the physicality of playing drums suited my personality. I had originally chosen to play guitar because I fancied myself more of a front person. Being in a band and playing music was way more important to me than what instrument I'd play, however, and I knew enough on guitar to help write songs because my songs only required three chords. By the time I got into Spitboy, I was a pretty experienced drummer and songwriter, the female Phil Collins of punk rock drummers. I played the drums, sang, and wrote about half the band's lyrics and some of the music too. I could even sing while drumming, which many people find astounding, only it isn't really, because when you're the one writing the songs, you can choose not to sing on parts of the song that would be too hard to sing on. Playing punk rock drums and singing does, however, take a great deal of cardio endurance and stamina. These things would not be difficult for me, but there were other things about playing drums that would be because I was not just a drummer, I was a female drummer. Being a female drummer requires a something else all together—patience.

"You hit hard for a girl."

I got that comment a lot from young men after nearly every show. The comment made me want to punch each guy who said it in the face. Instead, I'd just nod and focus on tearing down my kit. I could tell that some guys said it out of sheer astonishment at seeing a woman play drums and for others it was a pickup line or way to make conversation. I've had male friends tell me that they were afraid of me before they got to know me, and these annoying interactions with men could be one reason why I didn't go around smiling as much as the other Spitwomen, a reason why I might have had a "don't-fuck-with-me face." I was content not inviting annoying and often sexist comments from men after shows, so I sometimes kept to myself. On tour, I would be the band member most likely to sit in the van alone before a show, not always that interested in the male hardcore bands playing on the bill with us, and not that interested in making conversation over really loud music.

I had gotten somewhat used to the sexist attitudes about female musicians and people's weird fetishes for female drummers by the time I was in Spitboy, having started my first punk band in high school. Growing up in a small town, there weren't too many other punk kids, and rather than uniting around us, the punk boys who had vowed and failed to start their own band told us, "Girls can't play music."

"Who you telling we can't play music?" I said to one of them at a party, getting in his face, "I've been playing an instrument since I was in third grade."

Our biggest supporters turned out to be the local metal band guys. They were impressed by our songwriting and our grit. They told their friends about us and invited us to play with them at parties. They didn't try hitting on us and they didn't fetishize what we did. They just thought we were cool: high school girls playing punk rock music and writing their own songs, something they weren't even doing yet. While everyone else was busy calling me Sheila E., these metal guys praised my musicianship, even when I knew that it was still coming along. Maybe it was good that I had not learned about the drummer stereotypes before I learned to play. I may have let them inhibit how I felt about myself, doubting that I could play drums because I was female or write music and lyrics because I was just the drummer. And it's a good thing that those metal guys cheered us on.

Come Out with Your Hands Up

I n the 1990s, when a punk band wanted to play in Canada without a work permit, you had to take a chance. You had to devise a plan to convince border patrol agents that even though you looked like a band, had a van full of amps, guitars, and drums that you were not entering the country to play shows and make Canadian money. On Spitboy's first major US tour, having planned to drive as far north as Michigan for shows in Detroit and Flint, we decided, why not Canada too? Toronto was to be our first Canadian stop, but would we make it?

We had been on tour a couple of weeks already, so much of our merch had been sold, but there was still one box with some T-shirts and a box of seven-inches left in the back of the van under the loft. If a border patrol agent found the merchandise after seeing all of our equipment, she might deduce that we were crossing the border to perform, to make money—to work, essentially, and to do so without work permits, which is illegal. This is a kind of illegal similar to undocumented Mexicans working and making money in the United States, not that we made that connection at all.

Our Canadian tour contact, who really wanted us to play a show in Toronto, had told us what we had to do in order to avoid suspicion to assure border agents that we were not going to be making money in Canada, only spending it. We had heard stories from other touring bands too, so as we drove from Flint to the border, we worked out our plan. We stopped at a service station a couple of miles before the border crossing to put the plan into action. We all got out and went to the back of the van to pull out the merchandise, so we could hide it, and we rearranged all the equipment to hide the box of seven-inches that we didn't know what else to do with. When they asked, we decided that we'd say we were a band from the United States and that we had been on tour and were headed to Canada for a short vacation before driving all the way back to California.

Perhaps it was youthful optimism or pure naiveté, but we seemed pretty sure that we wouldn't be caught. We just thought we'd be turned away if our merchandise was discovered. We certainly didn't think we were taking some big risk, even after the run-in with the police in New Orleans, which had happened when we were on our way out of town. We had been driving around a bit lost, looking for the freeway, when we heard a loud voice over a bullhorn, ordering us to pull over. We had heard a couple of short siren squawks that we didn't think had anything to do with us, and once Karin, who was driving, realized that the sirens had been for us, she slowed the van to a stop. From the passenger seat, I remember thinking that it was weird that the cops wouldn't let us a drive ahead a bit to a stretch of road with a shoulder instead of the curve in the road alongside a guardrail not far from the freeway entrance we had been looking for. For some reason, they were in a big hurry to get us stopped on the side of the road and out of the van.

"Come out with your hands up!"

"They have us surrounded." Karin looked out the driver's side window, back to us, then back toward the window.

Paula and Adrienne sat frozen in the backseat.

"Come out with your hands up!"

With that we all scrambled out of the van, as if in a movie, with our hands up. The van *was* surrounded. Four, white, unmarked police cars and several police officers in SWAT gear semicircled around us with their guns drawn. I could hear the sound of cars whizzing down a freeway nearby.

"What are you doing in this neighborhood?"

We didn't know where we were, but I had noticed when we circled the block looking for the freeway that we were circling a run-down neighborhood, and I remembered seeing a few older black men sitting on a porch as we passed by. A couple of the officers were wearing vests that said "Drug Squad."

Of course, what else would a bunch of girls who looked like we did be doing in a neighborhood like that?

"We were looking for the freeway," Karin said an edge in her voice.

"Why were you circling around?" The lead officer shouted, still pointing his gun.

"We *were* looking for the freeway," I said, pissed.

Was it really necessary for Karin to repeat what she had just told him?

"What do you got in there?" The lead officer pointed to the back of the van.

"Musical equipment," Adrienne said, sounding as cooperative as she could.

"Open the back of the van, please."

"Yes, Officer." Adrienne walked to the back of the van with slow, careful steps, her boots crunching on gravel and dirt as she crept by.

I wanted to ask if that was even legal, searching our van like that, but I didn't. We just stood still, Karin, Paula, and I, avoiding any sudden movements, lined up just off the paved road, our backs to the guardrail.

We watched as Adrienne opened the double doors and as the lead officer and another officer took a look inside. The other officers kept their guns raised, pointing right at the rest of us, ready to shoot.

"Any weapons or contraband?" the lead officer asked before attempting to move anything in the back of the van.

"No, sir, just amps and guitars and drums. We're in band," Adrienne said. "We played a show here last night."

"Why were you circling around this neighborhood?"

I was getting impatient with that question.

"We told you that already. We're not from here. We were looking for the freeway," I said unable to hide my irritation, my arms now down at my sides.

"Don't get sassy with me, young lady."

I wanted to tell him to fuck off.

"The freeway entrance is right there." The lead officer pointed in the direction we were headed when they stopped us.

"Yes, sir, we know that. That's where we were headed when you pulled us over," Karin cut in.

The lead officer looked at the other cops and nodded his head. They lowered their guns.

"Okay, ladies, you can be on your way now."

All the cops turned and walked toward their cars, and we got back in the van and waited until the police cars surrounding the van were out of our way so we could get on the freeway and out of New Orleans as fast as we could without speeding or actually breaking any laws.

We couldn't believe we had been pulled over like that with guns drawn; still it didn't stop us from smuggling merchandise into Canada. It was just T-shirts and records, not drugs, or people, or fruit, or non-native plants, and it was before 9-11 when you could cross into Canada with just a driver's license, and we were Americans, so none of it felt like a big deal.

At the service station near the Canadian border, we put our merchandise smuggling plan into action. Each of us put on as many T-shirts as we could, starting with the smaller sizes on the bottom and layering with the larger sizes. It was either my idea to wear as many shirts as we could under our regular clothes or to repack our bags with as many T-shirt and seven-inches as we could at the bottom and our dirtiest clothes on the top; I can't quite remember which, but probably the latter. Both Karin and I had brought loose dresses to wear in the van, and so we put those on top. Paula and Adrienne put on their hoodies. Apparently not too worried that we were about to break a pretty serious law, we stood around outside of the van, pointing and laughing at each other, each a much puffier version of herself. It was nighttime, so it didn't look strange that we were a little bundled up.

Because we looked weird with our shades of different colored hair, because we were young, and because we were driving a van, we knew we'd be searched. We quieted down, no longer laughing or carrying on, while waiting in the line of cars, waiting to be questioned and sweating a little in our layers. I sat in the back of the van, hoping to go unnoticed in the dark. When it was our turn to hand over our identification and answer a few questions about where we were coming from and where we were headed, we were told to get out of the van. A male and female agent, wearing blue, opened the back of van and the side doors to have a look inside. They didn't spend much time searching the back of the van after they saw all the heavy equipment, but they did look carefully inside the van, opening our bags, which we had left out in the open to show that we didn't have anything to hide.

The four of us stood in a row alongside the van, as we had done while getting pulled over by the drug squad in New Orleans, and I could see beams from the border agents' flashlights sweeping the van. And even as serious as the situation now felt, I couldn't help smiling to myself as I waited with the other Spitwomen under the fluorescent lights of the border station, imagining the male and female agent opening our bags and finding dirty bras and bloodstained underwear, the dirtiest, sweatiest socks, and unused tampons spilling out. I imagined the female agent in her blue knee-length skirt thinking to herself, "dirty Americans." Once back in the van, I imagined them talking about us after we had zipped up our bags, and driven off into Canada to play two shows and to sell a couple hundred dollars' worth of merchandise, our feminine wiles and our cunning used not to lure and seduce, but instead to trick and deceive.

Shut Up and Play

66 Y ou guys have really improved."

People liked telling us that. They would use that word, too: "improved." It was supposed to be a compliment

"You're a lot tighter now."

I'd clench my jaw every time.

I had never heard anyone, especially a guy, saying that to another guy in a band. Imagine someone saying that to Neurosis or Econochrist.

But the comment that Spitboy got more often outside of the Bay Area was "shut up and play." It was only ever men who said it, and they'd shout it between songs when one of us was trying to say something, usually something about our lyrics. It was important to us to make sure our message wasn't totally lost over the hard, fast music. Punk boys in the Bay Area knew better than to say this, but they were the ones who liked telling us how much we had improved or how much they loved girl bands.

The shut-up-and-play comment usually only happened outside of the Bay Area and always got a lecture about respect by Adrienne or Karin, but a guy at a show in New Mexico improved on the insult, leaving us speechless.

We were on our first mini-tour, just the Southwest, and the show was in a garage in Albuquerque. Jesse, who rented the house with the garage had been putting on shows there for a while, but it was the kind of show that made us nervous to play: lots of drinking and violence in the pit. The garage had low ceilings, lined with pipes. Of course the crowd was made up of mostly men, and the majority of them in front of the stage were thrashing around, pushing each other, and not giving a shit about anything we had to say. After only the second song, Adrienne stopped us because one of the guys in the crowd had a bloody nose. When she asked if he was okay, he turned on her.

"We weren't fighting," he shouted and wiped at the blood streaming down his face. "You didn't have to stop playing!"

The front of his shirt was stained with blood, and blood was still trickling out of his nose.

Just as we started playing again, the same guy walked up toward Adrienne with a beer in his hand. He must have shaken it because when he opened it, beer and foam sprayed all in her face. She somehow didn't stop right then and beat his ass, which is what I might have done back then, given that I was the quickest to anger.

We continued playing, but the violent moshing continued, and after only one more song and partway through the song "Dysfunction," Jesse stopped the show.

"Ah, come on," someone yelled from the back, "just fucking play."

Adrienne announced again that we would not play because people weren't respecting the space or each other.

No one moved. Everyone seemed unsure what was really happening.

Then the voice from the back room rose up again.

"Hey, if you want to prove your womanhood, shut up and spread your legs or play."

All the heads in the room turned toward the voice.

"What did you say?" I asked over my vocal mic.

"Shut up and spread your legs or play."

The whole band was stunned. We had heard a lot of rude comments, been objectified, and shined on. We tried using humor, we tried to heckle back, and we tried educating people. But this comment, which was meant to humiliate us, set off a wildfire inside me.

I threw my sticks.

"Who said that? Who said that?" I screamed and I was on my feet, running into the crowd, shouting and waving my arms.

I only made it partway across the room before I was caught in a bear hug. It was Phil, the Paxston Quiggly guitar player, squeezing me as tight as he could so I couldn't get away.

"Fuck you!" I screamed at the town fool, swiping at the air, still locked in Phil's bear hug. We had met up with Paxston Quiggly for a couple of shows in New Mexico, the motherland of two of their members, because they knew a lot of people there and we thought it would be fun.

Neil, the bass player, my ex-boyfriend, was there now too, shouting in my ear over the commotion, "Todd, it's not worth it. Just forget it. That guy's dangerous. Phil heard he was on *America's Most Wanted.*"

I went limp in Phil's arms. It felt good to stop fighting, to be held right then. I reached up and put my arms around Neil's neck and the rest of the Spitboy and Paxston Quiggly gathered around. The singer, Bronwyn, and Kevin, the drummer of Paxston Quiggly, were there now too creating a barrier between us and the crowd.

The show was definitely over.

Even if we had planned on playing more, we wouldn't have been able to. All of our energy had been drained away. I could barely speak and Karin began to cry, which started the rest of the band crying along with her. Some people wandered away, not wanting to get involved, but others from the crowd stood around with concerned looks on their faces.

Once we all calmed down a bit, people who had come to see Spitboy play came up and offered to help us load our equipment or asked if they could buy a T-shirt. We probably sold more T-shirts that day than any band playing a garage ever.

When the crowd thinned out a bit more, a woman approached us.

"We're so sorry," she said.

"We hope you don't think everyone in New Mexico is like them," said the woman's boyfriend.

"No, we don't," Karin said, wiping at her nose with a tissue that someone had given her.

"Here," the woman said, pulling a wad of cash from her pocket.

The boyfriend took money from his pocket too and piled it onto the wad in his girlfriend's outstretched hand.

"It's just money, we know," said the woman, "but it's what we can do. We want to do something."

Someone else took money out of their pockets and handed it to Karin.

"Yeah, we want to do something," the woman said, reaching in and giving Karin a hug too.

It was a strange but extraordinary act of compassion, and it may have been this act that caused us to rethink our approach to hecklers, to the blatant sexism and disrespect that was not uncommon at our shows. I knew that I didn't want to ever get that angry again, even if it was deserved, and even after Jesse pulled us aside later and told us that in his six years of putting on shows in Albuquerque not one band ever stopped and confronted that particular group of guys who always came to shows to start trouble. We had been the first.

Still, we got tired of being called bitch and cunt. We knew that while we weren't going to play while people beat each other up in the mosh pit, we had to find better ways for dealing with harassment.

A couple of years later at a show in some side-room of a pizza joint in Fresno, some goon thought he'd try to get a rise out of us, but thanks to Karin, we didn't take the bait.

She had been trying to introduce a song when a faceless voice rose up out of the crowd.

"Ah, quit your bitching and play some music." It was a male voice, of course, and it came from the cowardly back corner of the long, dark, narrow room.

I could see Dominique, who was in the band now, look at Adrienne.

I waited, sticks poised in the air, ready to count the song off because sometimes the song alone was enough of an answer. But Karin had thought fast.

"Hey, you know what you need to do?" she said into microphone. "You need to go to the library and read a fucking book."

The crowd erupted in cheers. I saw a couple of women in the front row laughing as I clicked my sticks together, one, two, three, four. We heard later that the clown who had made the comment left before we finished playing the song.

Spitboy in Little Rock

One of the most memorable Spitboy shows, for me, was the show we played in Little Rock with Chino Horde outdoors during a spectacular summer rainstorm. It wasn't the playing itself that I remember so much; it was being in the audience, taking part in a moment, being a witness. I fell in love in Little Rock (something I only did once while on tour), but that's not the story I'm going to tell, though the two are definitely related.

We must have arrived in Little Rock early in the morning, or the night before we played in the afternoon by the river because we spent a lot of time at Burt Taggert's architectural marvel of a house, soaking up some genuine, old-fashioned Southern hospitality. Burt's mom was kind to us, but she clearly did not approve of our crumpled, fresh-out-of-the-van look and unshaven armpits, urging us to use her shower, "there's one here and another one down the hall," and rest up before we came to eat.

Rested and fed and chatted up, we made our way to the amphitheater where we'd play with Chino Horde and probably some other band too. Adding to the magic of the day, Burt and the rest of the guys doted on us quite a bit, asking if we needed to make any stops for anything we might need once back out on the road. I got the feeling that the Little Rock scene kids were this way with all bands that came through, but that we were getting the extra-special treatment because we were women, and not in the let-me-take-care-of-you-little-lady way; still, there was something sort of gentlemanly about it. And there had been, for quite some time, a strong connection between Little Rock and Bay Area bands, which probably started when Econochrist relocated to the Bay Area in the late 1980s, but these slightly younger Little Rock punk kids were more Ben Sizemore (quiet, thoughtful in action, and serious about their message) than Jon Sumrall (funny, wild, and sometimes out of control), though the Ben Sizemore comparison isn't quite right either. These guys were a whole new, kinder, gentler punk guy—there was nothing hard or threatening about them.

The sky was a hazy blue when we arrived at the large covered amphitheater, where we headlined since we were the touring band. We would have been happy playing anywhere on the bill, especially when we saw this beautiful spot—the lazy river, a bridge connecting the two sides of Little Rock on one side, and a large grassy area that spread out all around us. We had played churches, Elks lodges, basements, small all-ages clubs, and garages, but this was our first outdoor amphitheater and our first time in Little Rock.

To my surprise, the haziness in the sky had turned to clouds as people began arriving for the show, and by the time Chino Horde began to play, the rain was coming down heavy. The large, covered amphitheater stage held all the bands and all the punk kids who came out, and we all managed to stay mostly dry. I had never seen or heard of Chino Horde before the tour, but I couldn't take my eyes off them as soon as they took the stage. Depending on how tired or overstimulated I felt on tour, I would sometimes sit in the van and read before playing. I didn't usually get nervous before playing, but I did often need to gather myself quietly before playing, and sometimes the van was the only quiet place to go. But sometimes there were bands like Chino Horde who gave you energy, made you excited to get up there after them and participate in the moment, and that's how I felt on that day. It didn't matter that the rain was coming down. It only added intensity to the band onstage, their performance punctuated by claps of thunder and flashes of lightning.

At one point during the Chino Horde set, with Burt, and Steve, and Jason all at their mics, the rain started coming down sideways, wetting one side of the stage. I remember looking from Karin and Adrienne and Paula and to the suddenly dark sky and the rain all around us. They looked worried too, for we couldn't be sure that Chino Horde or the rest of us wouldn't be electrocuted. It seemed that Mother Nature was trying to match the energy onstage, or even demanding that Chino Horde keep up, because the further Chino Horde got into their set, the harder it rained. I had never seen such a thing before, a group so intent on playing their music that what seemed to me a dangerous electrical storm was of no consequence. And for a moment I didn't want them to stop. The weather, the music, the young men playing their hearts out in front of us, the whole thing took my breath away.

And just when I didn't think I could take any more of the frightening weather and Chino Horde's intensity, Burt announced their last song and, just like that, the rain slowed, the clouds parted, and the sun burst through, lighting the sky. The audience couldn't help turning its attention to the sudden change overhead, to the sun shining down again on the bridge, creating a reflection on the water. I remember looking at Karin, and Paula, and Adrienne, wide-eyed, relieved, and in disbelief that such a thing could happen, at what we had just witnessed. Then as Burt, and Steve, and Jason strummed their final notes, and David hit his cymbals the final time, a glittering rainbow fanned out across the whole sky.

Race, Class, and Spitboy

My Grandma Delia hadn't been expecting us, so her short hair was a troll doll mess, she didn't have her eyebrows drawn on, and she wasn't wearing any lipstick. But I figured she'd be home, being as it was a Sunday evening and she was seventy-five.

"Mi'ja!" She looked confused and surprised when she opened the door and saw me there with the other Spitwomen all in mostly black, dirty jean shorts over leggings, boots or heavy Doc Marten shoes, tattoos, and faded tank tops.

Spitboy had been playing a series of shows in the LA area, including a big festival in Long Beach, and we were on our way back to the Bay Area. I couldn't drive past my Grandma Delia's East LA freeway exit without stopping, and I wanted the Spitwomen to meet her. A tough old broad, she speaks with an accent, speaks and cusses in both English and Spanish, and was born and raised in the United States after her parents came from Mexico during the revolution in 1918. In her own proud-to-be-American, culturally Mexican, don't-tell-me-what-to-do-I-can-make-up-my-own-mind way, she was and is a feminist too.

I gave her a big hug in the doorway and explained that we had been playing music in the area and that we were on our way home. Her house was just off the freeway in Lincoln Heights. As we turned onto Workman Street, I had pointed out General Hospital where I was born and explained that this was East LA, the place my family is from.

"Do you want me to make you something to eat?"

"No, Grandma, we can't stay long. I just wanted you to meet everyone."

"Come in, come in." She opened the door wider so we could all pass by. "Where are my manners?"

The Spitwomen lingered on the porch behind me, uncharacteristically quiet, even Adrienne, who always smiled and introduced herself to everyone anywhere we went. Once we made our way inside the house and once someone shut the heavy metal screen door behind her, Karin scanned the room. The way her eyes fell over every item made me aware of just how many knickknacks, photographs, and wall hangings lined the small combined living room/dining room, including the one that said, "Home is where you can scratch where it itches." Adrienne stood in faux-leather pants with her hands clasped in front of her, and Paula smiled politely.

"Grandma, this is Karin." I pointed at Karin. "She plays guitar in the band. This is Adrienne; she sings, and Paula plays bass."

"Hello, please sit down," Grandma said, for all three of them had filed around behind the coffee table in front of the couch.

I could tell that Grandma Delia didn't know what else to say.

They sat down on the couch; Karin on one edge, her head near the macramé plant hanger with the peace lily spilling out of it. She had the same expression on her face during a discussion that we had a couple of different times driving to shows. It was a discussion about my family, or really just a series of questions.

"You and your brother and your sister all have different fathers?"

"Yes, we each have a different father," I'd say, not sure why the question, one that she had asked me before, made me uncomfortable. Karin, Paula, and Adrienne's parents were all still married, maybe not all happily, but Karin's parents were actually very nice and not dysfunctional at all, the kind of family that owned an Audi and a commuter car, had straight teeth, and didn't lose their tempers.

"So each of you has a different last name?" She furrowed her brow.

Feeling like I should defend my mom, I'd explain how she got pregnant with me in high school but left my dad when I was eight months old because he abused her.

This was something I figured that she'd understand since we had written a song about domestic violence.

"She got together with my brother's dad who helped her leave my dad, but they never married and were only together for a couple of years. Later, my mom married my sister's dad and had my sister."

Since we didn't think marriage was cool at all, I added that my mom was no longer married to my sister's dad, or anyone else, that she had sworn off marriage forever.

I followed Grandma, who wore what she called a pair of joggers and a faded cat sweatshirt, to the kitchen, so we could chat a minute and because no one else seemed to have anything to say. When it was warm she always wore a housedress.

"How are you, Grandma?" I asked once were in the kitchen.

"I'm fine; you know, getting older every day." She ran her finger through her hair and smiled. Her nails looked freshly manicured, oval-shaped and bright red.

She handed me two glasses filled with water so I could help her carry them, one of narrow ribbed glass and the other of tin, the kind from the seventies, each in the set painted a different color and designed to keep your Kool-Aid really cold.

The Spitwomen were still sitting quietly when my grandma and I got back into the front room and handed each a glass of water. Karin was still looking around the room with her nose in the air; Paula, who always wore her short hair in a ponytail, looked as if she was trying to think of something to say; Adrienne was sitting with her hands folded in her faux-leather lap.

"Sit down, mi'ja," Grandma motioned to her chair, beside which sat her basket of embroidery projects. I could see that she was working on a design of a Mexican woman carrying a jug of water on her shoulder.

I sat down, and each of the Spitwomen took a sip of her water and set her glass down on the coffee table without saying a word. They were never this quiet, ever. I didn't know what to do. Grandma read my anxiety and tried to fill the awkward silence herself.

"You girls must be tired, driving all that way."

They all nodded.

"You see that picture there," she said, pointing to a black metal shelf by the door, "That's Michelle's mom and dad when they were in high school."

I winced when she called me Michelle because they never called me that; they only ever called me Todd.

"They were at a dance. Your mom looks so pretty, don't you think so, mi'ja?"

I always thought she looked much older than sixteen or seventeen, with her hair in a sort of a ratted, late-sixties, beehive bun. And my dad, short, dark skinned, with thick black hair; I looked like him with my hair cropped close to my head the way I was wearing it then, in a sort of Mia Farrow *Rosemary's Baby* haircut.

I nodded at my grandma and smiled, but I felt sad. I didn't know what to say now either and that just made it worse.

Stopping had not been a good idea at all. We should have stayed on I-5. I should not have suggested that we veer off into the second-largest Mexican city in the world. I had made everyone uncomfortable, and now I was outside of my body, seeing my adored Grandma and her shabby East LA home, which I had always found tidy and comforting, her knickknacks, which they probably called tchotchkes, and all her family photos of Mexicans, and now myself through different eyes, and I didn't like it one bit.

When we left LA, we didn't talk a lot in the van on the long drive over the Grapevine on I-5. There was plenty to say, but I would have had to find the words and the courage to say what was on my mind. I didn't have it, nor would I for a long time, but it would fester inside me like an angry tumor that would grow and grow until I couldn't pretend it wasn't there anymore.

The Spitboy Rule

S pitboy had a rule: no boyfriends on tour. It was a good rule, but it turned out there were ways around it.

We didn't take anyone with us on our first tour, boyfriends or otherwise. That may have been a mistake, but we wanted to prove that we could do it all: write our own songs, play our own instruments, drive the van, navigate the interstates with a paper map, unload our own equipment, and change our own tires (and in only a matter of minutes). Paula, our bass player, even fixed the van when it broke down. She spent hours and hours with her head in the engine in Missoula, Montana, oil on her face and up to the tattoo on her freckled shoulder. I sat in the van (the engines could only be accessed from inside the van) with her handing her tools for as long as I could stand it, not quite sure what she was so grumpy about, not realizing at first that she felt the way I did whenever we finished a set and young women would come to tell us how much we meant to them, and I was stuck tearing down my drums and getting them out of the way of the next band, while the others basked in the praise.

Paula's dad had taught her to work on cars when she expressed an interest, and her know-how made it possible for us to get across the United States and back without spending what little money we made from shows and merchandise on van repairs more than twice. We did have to get the blue van repaired in Wyoming. For some reason, we always broke down in Wyoming; Wyoming was Spitboy's Bermuda Triangle.

Touring all on our own with no roadies, without anyone who wasn't in the band to help drive that first time around was hard, but it was important for us to know that we could. We were one of the only all-female punk bands playing straight forward hardcore, no jangly chords, reverb, or feminine harmonies for us, just the driving sounds of chunky bar chords, thumping bass lines, rapid-fire drum beats, and Adrienne's warbly growl. And being women who spent a lot of time together even when we weren't touring, our menstrual cycles would often sync up. It got to where we'd each start our period within a day a day or so of the other. We got to a show in Minot, North Dakota, just before the first band was about to take the stage, which made the show's promoter really nervous, but three of us were on our periods at the same time. We had to stop every twenty or thirty minutes at a different dirty roadside gas station bathroom on our already long drive from Chicago or wherever we were coming from. We apologized to the nervous promoter and told him the truth—three out of the four of us were on our period and we had to stop a lot. He didn't need to hear any more. "That's okay," he said, waving his hand in the air like a little boy. He'd probably never heard that excuse from a band before. Having someone else to worry about driving on those days might have made things easier. I know I wasn't a steady or efficient driver while suffering from a bad case of cramps.

The long late-night drives to a new city, or in some cases new state, those were the worst without a roadie. We'd have to leave for these long, all-night drives right after the show in order to make it in time for the next, the next day, usually resulting in our arrival at our new destination sometime in the morning. Having no place to go meant we had to find a safe place to park and sleep in the van. Having one more person to share driving shifts would have just been a smart and safe thing to do. Instead, one of us would drive, another would try to stay awake and navigate, while two of us slept in our sleeping bags on the futon on the loft built for that purpose behind the middle row of seats. I had the ability to wake up after four or so terrible hours of sleep, stumble into whatever gas station we had stopped at, buy a cup of the worst coffee in America and some water, take a no-doze, and get back in the van and drive. Once back on the interstate, I'd listen to whatever CDs I wanted to, sing along quietly, and keep my eyes peeled for weird construction cones, potholes, wild animals, and cops. The driving part never bothered me much; it was the fatigue the next morning, trying to get back to sleep after driving four or so hours straight, the sun coming up, and the rest of the band one-by-one with it.

The no-boyfriends-on-tour rule went out the van window on our European tour in 1993. We had no choice but to bring a lot of people, a whole entourage. First off, we had to hire drivers because none of us had driver's licenses to drive overseas, and since Paula was now dating the best, most famous roadie in the punk scene, Pete the Roadie, we had to bring him too. And we brought Jon Hiltz, Born Against drummer, who Karin had always had a shine for, to help sell merchandise. While logical to break the no-boyfriends-on-tour rule for the European tour, the rule itself made even more sense. With Paula off with Pete, and Karin snogging with Jon in the dark on long drives, things felt a little less unified. Men did change things. Some of us now had a person with her that was just her own, while others didn't. I didn't. And Adrienne didn't either.

Boyfriends on tour in Europe did change the dynamic, but it never changed what we had onstage every night. People often commented on our live performances and the way we connected with one another and the audience. It probably helped that we all wrote lyrics. Adrienne always sang lead, and if she were singing lead on a song that I wrote, I would sing with her. This sort of collaboration worked the same way with songs written by Karin, Paula, and later Dominique. Jon Hiltz said that we were the most positive, supportive band he ever met. His experience in his own band had apparently been somewhat fraught, but I could see how difficult it could be to get along on tour with some people, away from the comforts of home, the stress of the long drives, the fatigue, and the close quarters. Though it came somewhat naturally for Spitboy to make an effort and not take one another for granted and to accept certain quirks we hadn't noticed at home—Paula was moody at times; Karin was very good at getting her own needs met, I was too often standoffish and needy; and Adrienne loved to socialize so much that she had trouble getting to certain band duties like tearing down equipment and selling merchandise. Accepting these quirks was the right the thing to do and it never affected our live performances. On the other hand, if being in a band is like a marriage (and trust me, it is), then playing live is the sex, which makes playing live easy. It's the payoff, the place where we might even be able to fake it, but Spitboy never faked it. We genuinely liked one another and admired one another in many ways, too.

Karin earned much admiration during and after our first show in France. It happened about midway through a sluggish, we're-tired-after-touring-all-week-with-Citizen Fish-and-we-just-got-off-the-ferry set of songs. A guy started shouting something from the crowd, something like, "Enlevez vos chemises! Enlevez vos chemises," meaning take off your shirts! As soon as he said it, a woman standing at the front of the low stage began waving her hands wildly and yelling to us in English, wanting to tell us what he had said, but Karin (fluent in French since college) had understood. And instead of launching into the next song, she stepped up to her microphone and calmly, almost politely, cussed the guy out in his own language. For a second, the room went almost totally silent. Then it erupted into a loud volley of cheering and laughter, especially by the women in the crowd. No one had been expecting anything like that at all.

In part, it was this sort of admiration of one another and all that each of us was capable of that caused us to make the no-boyfriends-on-tour rule in the first place. I know I never wanted divided loyalties to interfere with or change any of it. But after the first US tour, we were never able to fully abide by the boyfriend rule, though it was there in the back our minds, reminding us to not pick at the quirks, to remain united, to make the most of each quick stop in a different city, and in the case of Europe, sometimes a different country each day. Together we played to five hundred people in Rome; walked over the spooky, beautiful Charles Bridge in Prague; gazed up at the Gaudí Museum in Barcelona after dark; and ate pizza fresh out of a backyard brick oven overlooking an olive farm in Toscano, Italy. I never felt alone or divided on days like that, and I wasn't.

Adrienne onstage with Citizen Fish, ABC No Rio,
New York, 1994. Photo: Chris Boarts Larson.

The author at McGreggors, Chicago, 1992. Photo: Karoline Collins.

T.D.S PRESENTS

BENEFIT FOR CONTRA COSTA ALTERNATIVE SCHOOL FEB. 29 1:00 AT THE PARADIGM

9029 SAN LEANDRO ST. OAK.

ALL AGES

WENDY-O-

BLISTER
ECONOCHRIST
SPECIALFORCES
FILTH
PAXSTONQUIGGLY
SPITBOY
GRIMPLE
GAGORDER
SINISTER &
+ BUCKY'S SIX XIS

e 2

a don't want to miss...

donation...madison

SPITBOY

WITH G.O.P.

AT TRENDZ

WEDNESDAY MAY 27

ALL AGES !!!

MUSIC BEGINS
AT 10:00 PM

FIRST
9 PM

SPITBOY—LP
Having seen SPITBOY play around the Bay Area the last year or so I knew this would be a good record. I wasn't prepared for its absolute greatness. Musically, it's mid-tempo punk rock with angst/raw vocals. The lyrics reflect what it's like to be a woman in 20 century America and to deal with rape, sexism and fear of the streets daily. I think this record will encourage quite a few women to start bands of their own. Truly inspiring. (MM) (Lookout Records)

U.S. tour, 1992.

U.S. tour 1994. Photo: David Sine.

U.S. tour 1994. Photo: David Sine.

The author at Olde West Studios, recording session with
Kevin Army, circa 1992. Photo: John Lyons.

U.S. tour. Photo: David Sine.

Adrienne at Olde West Studios. Photo: John Lyons.

Karin and guitar. Photo: John Lyons.

Karin, Kevin Army, and Paula in the studio. Photo: John Lyons.

Spitboy at the University of Montana, 1992.

Spitboy, Arizona, 1991.

Spitboy at 924 Gilman. Photo: John Lyons.

The author and a pig in Italy.

Spitboy with Phil
of Citizen Fish.
Photo: John Hiltz.

ANTWERP
PUNK-ROCK
FESTIVAL '93

met :

VOID SECTION
DRITTE WAHL (DDR)
SPITBOY (USA)
INSTIGATORS (UK)
JASON RAWHEAD
DIRT UK

ZONDAG 2 MEI 1993
HOF TER LO A'PEN

café **TSJAPLIN**
Zaal voor TD's fuiven concerten
enkel verenigingen !!!

Noordersingel 28. Borgerhout

Deuren : 14.00 h.

VVK ADRESSEN:

Brabo, netrophone (A'pen)
music mania (Gent)

Hoventakelaan 227
DUDGE

Spitboy in the English countryside.

The author at Buckingham Palace.

Producciones ZAMBOMBO presenta:
FESTIVAL-HOMENAJE A RAFAELA APARICIO
Con 2 grupos de chicas:

SPITBOY , Punk-rock, San Francisco, USA
LA NUBE , Las L7 Zaragozanas

Jueves 8 Abril , 20 pm. SALA-BAR PIRAMYS

SPITBOY

INVITACION

```
.......SPITTOUR........
MARCH 27  ARRIVE HEATHROW: 12:30PM
          "FISHBOY PART OF TOUR"
       28  BRISTOL: "FLEECE & FIRKIN"
       29  MANCHESTER: "BAND ON THE WALL"
       30  LEEDS: "DUCHESS OF YORK"
       31  SUNDERLAND: "RIVER WEAR"
APRIL   1  WIGA".
        2  KIDDERMINSTER: "MARKET TAVERN"
        3  BERKHAMPSTEAD: "GOING UNDERGROUND"
        4  LONDON: "THE SWAN"
        5  FERRY TO CALAIS. FRANCE (5AM DEPARTURE)
           SHOW @ SUBURB OUTSIDE PARIS
        6  TOULOUSE. FRANCE
           CONTACT: ARNO HUFTIER    (#3320470031)
        7  LLODIO. ALAVA (BASQUE.SPAIN)
           SHOW @ "COLLECTIVO TXIXARRA"
           CONTACT: ARNESTO NAVARRO
                    P.O. BOX 153
                    LLODIO, ALAVA
                    SPAIN 01400    (#3446723930)
        8  BASQUE. SPAIN
           SHOW: PARTY
           (SAME CONTACT AS #7)
        9  BARCELONA, SPAIN
           SHOW @ "COMMUNICADO"
           CONTACT: JOSE-ANTONIO    (#3476217437)
       10  LYON. FRANCE
           SHOW @ SQUAT
           CONTACT: MAIE/ERIC       (#3378305152)
                    23 PIACE TAFIN  (#3378305728)
                    59300 VALINCINNAS, FRANCE
       11  MILANO, ITALY
           SHOW @ "CSOA LEONCAVALLO"
                    VIA LEONCAVALLO
                    22 MILANO, ITALY  (#02/26140287) DANIELE/FRANCO
       12  FAENZA. ITALY
           SHOW @ "IL CLANDESTINO"
                    VIALE BACCARINI
                    21/a FAENZE, ITALY  (#0546/681327) MORENA
       13  ROMA. ITALY
           SHOW @ "CSOA FORTE PRENESTINO"
                    VIA F. DEL PINO
                    21 ROMA, ITALY    (#06/896541) CARMELO
       14  NO SHOW....DRIVE FROM HELL OVER THE ALPS^^^^^^
       15  ZURICH, SWITZERLAND
       16  BADDURKHEIN, GERMANY
           SHOW @ "HOUSE DE UNIDIN" (YOUTH CENTER)
           CONTACT: CORY FOR GIGS APRIL 15-28  (#49621559742) OR (#49621553707)
       17  NAGOLD, GERMANY
           SHOW @ YOUTH CENTER
       18  ESCH-ACETTE, LUXEMBURG
           SHOW @ SQUAT?? (POSSIBLY ELSEWHERE IS SQUAT CLOSES)
       19  FRANKFURT, GERMANY
           SHOW @ "BOCKDENHEIM" (YOUTH CENTER)
       20  PRAHA. CHEZ.
           SHOW @ YOUTH CENTER (YES, A HELLISH DRIVE TO & FRO)
       21  ESSEN. GERMANY
           SHOW @ "OVERHAUSEN"
       22  BERLIN. GERMANY
           SHOW @ "S.E.K." (IN FRIEDRICHSHAIN)
       23  WOLFSBURG, GERMANY
           SHOW @ YOUTH CENTER
       24  BREMEN. GERMANY
           SHOW @ "WIERSCHLOSS"
           CONTACT: CHANGE MUSIC (#9421702342)
                    SIELPFAD 11
                    2800 BREMEN 1, GERMANY
       25  HANNOVER. GERMANY
           SHOW @ "KORN"
       26  ALBURG. GERMANY
           SHOW @ "1,000 SIYD"
       27  HAMBURG. GERMANY
           SHOW @ "THE FLORA SQUAT"
       28  GOTTINGEN. GERMANY
           SHOW @ YOUTH CENTER
       29  AMSTERDAM, HOLLAND
           SHOW @ (HOPEFULLY) A SQUAT
       30  ZUTPHEN. HOLLAND
           SHOW @ "THE DEBARIK" (YOUTH CENTER)
MAY     1  YPRES, BELGIUM
           SHOW @ "VORT-N-VIS"  (HUGE ALL DAY FESTIVAL)
           BRUNO (#3291336862)/(#3257334800)
        2  ANTWERPEN, BELGIUM
           SHOW @ HUGE FESTIVAL/ ALL DAY
           HERWIN (#32036468032)
```

Paula/Pete
25 B GEORGE ST.
WARMINSTER
WILTSHIRE- WESSEX

Spitboy with Ross Gardiner in New Zealand, 1995. Photo: Karoline Collins.

Ross Gardiner at the Spitboy wall in New Zealand, 1995. Photo: Karoline Collins.

Spitboy with Clint Chapman in Sydney, 1995. Photo: Karoline Collins.

Spitboy with a koala, Australia, 1995. Photo: Karoline Collins.

Dominique and Michelle with punk rock koala. Photo: Karoline Collins.

Instant Girl in the making, Sydney Opera
House, 1995. Photo: Karoline Collins.

Pacific Rim tour 1995. Photo: Karoline Collins.

Spitboy in Japan. Photo: Karoline Collins.

The author in Japan, 1995. Photo: Karoline Collins.

Tattoos in Japan.

Spitboy with Japanese crew, 1995. Photo: Karoline Collins.

The author with drummer of Nature Apology Arised,
Japan 1995. Photo: Karoline Collins.

Fish or Fugazi

W hen we were touring overseas in spring of 1993, Fugazi requested we play with them when they came to the Bay Area. Karin got word of the request when she called home from the road. Being the biggest Fugazi fan in the band, and definitely inspired by their guitar sound, she beamed when she told us the news, and we talked about it a lot, driving from one country to another in a day the way you can do in Europe. It was a huge honor to be asked to open for Fugazi, and we knew it was likely our only chance to play with the band that wrote "Suggestion," one of the best feminist punk songs ever, and a song that (along with and our collective personal experiences, of course) inspired our song "The Threat."

Even though I wasn't ever straight edge, I had actually been a big Minor Threat fan and had listened to them growing up in Tuolumne.

When I think of Minor Threat, I automatically see myself walking down a hot road with no sidewalks to Bitch Fight guitarist Nicole Lopez's house, singing, "Out of step with the world." Nicole, who was usually straight edge, had turned me on to Minor Threat. Growing up in a home wracked by drug and alcohol abuse, I appreciated their message about the destruction of substance abuse and heeded their warnings in my own quest for moderation.

Spitboy was really disappointed to have to pass on the chance to play with Fugazi, to play for them. I fantasized about being onstage at the Fort Mason Center, Ian MacKaye looking up at us lovingly from the front of the stage, nodding his head as we played. My own disappointment was quelled by the fact that we had spent the first week of our European tour in England with punk icons Dick, Trotsky, and Phil of Citizen Fish, also known as members of Subhumans, another band that I listened to incessantly in Tuolumne on my 1970s turntable in my coffin-like attic bedroom. "I don't want to die/I don't want to d-d-d-d-die!" Dick's distinctly English-accented singing voice is one of those singing voices that I will always associate with my teenage years, growing up in a small dirt town that felt as far away from England as it could get. A huge Clash fan, I had dreamt often of traveling to England, but it felt nothing more than a fantasy, as I wasn't sure I'd ever get out of Tuolumne, or get out of there in one piece.

Driving between shows in England, I'd often stare at the rolling green hills out the small window of Trotsky's van. During one particular drive, I sat in the back chatting with Phil as Trotsky drove, since it was his van. Paula sat with Pete, Karin with Jon, and Dick, Jasper, and Adrienne must have been sleeping when I told Phil about what a fan I had been of Subhumans.

"I saw you guys play at the Farm in San Francisco in 1986."

"Really? You were at that show?" He looked surprised.

"I was. Do you remember it?"

"Of course I remember it." He grinned.

They had played with Dead Kennedys and Frightwig, and shows at the Farm were usually memorable, big, sweaty, and violent. Skinheads would turn out to make trouble, and there was security in the entryway and onstage. The stage was high and there was always lots of stage diving and moshing, and Suzy, Nicole, Nicole's mom, and I would wiggle our way through the crowd to the front of the stage, so we could both be close and sort of out of the way of the mosh pit and below the stage divers who soared over our heads. The stage was so high that I had to stand on tiptoes to even get a glimpse of Trotsky on drums. Dick paced, swinging his head back and forth right above us.

I told Phil about how I hadn't grown up in the Bay Area, that I had grown up in a small town, and how much of an effort it took to see a punk show or even buy a punk record.

"We weren't going to miss it—Subhumans in San Francisco."

"Yeah?" Phil said, his grin turning into a full-on smile, not at all embarrassed that I was going all fangirl on him.

"We drove three hours to get there after school and three hours back after the show."

"Really?" He was smiling even more now, as he often did, all teeth showing, his eyebrows arching high and wide.

I nodded.

"Did you hear that, Trotsky? Todd here saw us play in 1986 at the Farm in San Francisco. Drove three hours just to get to the show."

Trotsky turned his head and flashed the smile that always made the Spitwomen swoon, taking his eyes off the road, and turning back again.

"That's something, that's really something," Phil said, shaking his head.

And it really was. I had only been living in the Bay Area for six years. I was a preschool teacher, making something like five or six dollars an hour, and I was in a band touring Europe, traveling with members of a band that I had listened to feeling isolated and alone growing up in hick town. I was being served black tea by Phil or Trotsky of the Subhumans and now Citizen Fish every day at tea time and slamming away on my drums onstage every night. I had my first crumpet with honey and butter at Phil's house, and the first time Jasper, the Citizen Fish bass player, took my tea order, I couldn't believe that he'd fixed it just the way I liked it.

"Todd, how do you take your tea?" he asked.

"You're going to make my tea?" I couldn't believe it.

"Righto." Jasper's accent was a bit different than the rest of the band.

"Two sugars, no cream." I wondered how it would taste.

We were staying at someone's house, friends of Citizen Fish. It was some kind of country cottage, decorated to look like one, complete with table linens, teacups, and saucers. We must have been quite a sight all in black and gray, ripped jeans, studs, and band T-shirts, sitting around on antique chairs waiting for tea in china cups.

Once the water was boiled and the tea prepared, Jasper, who had taken other orders too, came back with my tea. I thanked him and waited for him to turn around before I took a sip or ducked into the kitchen to add more sugar like I thought I might have to, but I didn't have to at all. The tea was perfect, probably the best cup of tea that I had ever had. I leaned back in the brocade settee and sipped my tea, savoring the whole cup.

It was hard to have to turn down playing a show with Fugazi, but being doted on by Citizen Fish, stopping in the countryside to stretch our legs and kick the soccer ball with them, drinking my first Tetley beer, watching Trotsky play drums up close six nights in a row, and getting to know dear Phil, who I saw play guitar the first time at the Farm in 1986, in jolly old England hadn't been hard at all.

Pete the Roadie

I t didn't seem very punk rock to me to have roadies, to be waited on by people hired to help, so when we had to find people to help us on tour, I felt a little reluctant about it. My reluctance about hired help was magnified because I'm a woman, the oldest daughter of a single mother, expected to anticipate the needs of others, and not the other way around.

To be clear, no one that I knew in a punk band considered roadies just the hired help. Roadies were usually friends who knew a thing or two about guitars, amps, and drums and didn't mind helping the band lug shit around, and often for no more than the opportunity to travel. But when Paula started dating Pete the Roadie, Spitboy had instant access to an actual professional roadie, a man who had dedicated his life to touring with bands and practically crafting the punk rock roadie code for punk rock roadies who admired and looked up to him, even trained with him. Pete, and roadies like him, were not unlike those in other service jobs who took serving others seriously. In fact, I thought of Pete the Roadie many years later when I read Barbara Ehrenreich's opinions about what it means to serve in her book *Nickel and Dimed*. Unlike Ehrenreich, though, who worked as a waitress and hotel maid and then went back to her real life to write about it, being a roadie and serving others is Pete the Roadie's real life.

Pete seemed to believe that his primary job was to serve artists, to make it easier for them to make the music that he loved and to spread the ideas that he believed in. He did what he did without the glory of actually being in the band. I admired this code, being a woman whose life had, in large part, been about serving others, helping my mom take care of my brother and sister, and in my job as a preschool teacher where all I did was take care of small children who couldn't take care of themselves (not to mention their anxious parents). But when applied to me, it felt decadent. I didn't feel comfortable being served. Still, none of that mattered to Pete. All that mattered to him was that my drums were set up properly and nothing moved out of place when I played them.

When we played live, Pete would kneel at the side of the stage, halfway between the drum kit and the amps, in his grungy jeans and work boots, a roadie tool attached to his belt for easy access. Ready to jump into action, he'd watch for me to nod in the direction of my hi-hat if it was sliding out of place or the bass drum pedal, which often came loose by my furious pounding. When I nodded, Pete would come running to fix whatever was out place, his fingers always in danger of getting munched by some moving part on the drum hardware, a consequence that he'd gladly accept if it allowed me to finish out whatever song we had been playing uninterrupted.

During one show in Prague, our only show in the Czech Republic (a country that had split from Slovakia just that year), my bass drum pedal went clean through the head of the bass drum of the set I was borrowing from one of the opening acts. In England, while touring with Citizen Fish, I had played Trotsky's set, and Karin and Paula had used the Citizen Fish amps, as we had been unable to bring our large pieces of equipment over on the plane, just guitars, cymbals, and my snare drum. Not having my own kit scared me at first. Would I be able to play someone else's drum set, a different set each night? Touring definitely required a new kind of flexibility. Still, I hadn't actually worried so much about breaking someone else's kit. The head of the Prague drum set must have been worn already because I could feel it give way early in the set. I looked down at it, wondering if I could see a crack, and when I looked back up, Pete had stood from his keeling position, his eyes trained on me, waiting for a cue. By the end of the song, the pedal had gone straight through the head and there wasn't another. Pete had watched the mallet slice through the head and was at my side with a solution when I thought we may not be able to even go on. As I signaled to the band what was going on, Pete moved my drum stool out of the way, disconnected the foot pedal from the bass drum, and set about unscrewing the head from the drum using the drum key normally attached to his other tools on his belt loop.

"Don't worry, drums," he said to me, looking over his shoulder on his hands and knees in front of the kit, "I'll have this sorted right quick."

In addition to his dedication to the service, Pete also really loved the communal feel of being on the road, the friendships that developed, the habits, the fast pace, and the inside jokes. Pete rarely called me by name. He'd usually call me "drummer" or "drums," especially when I was onstage. He called Adrienne "singer," and he called Paula "Mrs. Roadie," as he still does today. Pete also took it upon himself to make sure we had drinks if we wanted them, and he memorized what we liked to drink and when. He knew I was homesick too, missing my Little Rock boyfriend Jason, so he'd sit with me while I drank my glass of Tetley once we finished playing and he had the drums torn down and the equipment sorted and put away.

The movie *Wayne's World* had just come out, and we had all seen it because, like *Spinal Tap*, it parodied rock musicians, who we both represented and were rebelling against at the same time. Somewhere early in the tour, Pete and I began making *Wayne's World* jokes, trying to make the other laugh harder with each new joke. But nothing made me laugh harder than when Pete the Roadie, who's not known for being the sexiest guy in town, his punk band T-shirts tucked into his road-dingy jeans for quicker access to his roadie tools, arched his pelvis toward my hi-hat and said, "Sha-wing, hi-hat."

Watching him on his knees in front of my drum set in Prague, feeling bad that I'd destroyed somebody's set, I felt like I should do something to help Pete fix the bass drum head. But there wasn't much I could do but watch in awe as Pete, pit-crew-fast, pulled the rim off the drum, turned the head 180 degrees, put the rim back on, tightened all eight tension rods, and duct-taped the hole that was now at the top of the drum instead of near the bottom where it would be hit by the mallet.

When he was finished attaching the pedal, he stood and wiped his hands on his pants.

"Party on, bass drum," he said with a big smile.

This cracked me up extra hard, given that I had just broken someone else's bass drum head, and Pete's duct tape job had given it more life, though much altered.

I wanted to hug him but there was no time.

My mirth over the repaired drum head and getting to finish our set didn't last long, because after the show we learned that most people who attended the show had paid a week's wages to get in. We were sitting in the tour organizer's gray, utilitarian-looking high-rise apartment. It was hard to hear. All I could think of was that I should have paid for the drum head and Spitboy should have played for free. If we had known this in advance, I want to believe that we would have done the right thing, even though Prague had been a super long drive from East

Berlin—"a hellish drive," Karin had written on our itinerary. Though the prostitutes all along the highway on our way there should have been some kind of clue that the recent reunification of East and West Germany, and the breaking apart of the former Czechoslovakia had not resulted in any kind of instant economic prosperity.

I thought about Prague and all its haunting beauty and grayscale block housing on the long drive back to East Berlin, driving by the sex workers once again, probably the same women standing by the side of the road on the way there. I thought about the people who spent a week's wages just to see us play and wondered if it had been worth it, and how naïve we had been going there. I hoped that the drum head that Pete had doctored with duct tape would last.

My Body Is Mine

When we released our *Mi Cuerpo Es Mío* seven-inch, a riot grrrl from Olympia accused Spitboy of cultural appropriation. The riot grrrl had ties to the Bay Area, and she was white. Maybe she really believed the accusation. Maybe cultural appropriation was a new concept to her, one that she learned at Evergreen College and felt applied to us, or maybe she was just pissed off at Spitboy because we had distanced ourselves from her movement. She objected to our use of Spanish for the title of our record and accused us of stealing from someone else's culture, in particular the words "mi cuerpo es mío," which translates to "my body is mine."

Apparently my body was invisible.

Mi Cuerpo Es Mío, Spitboy's third release, followed our self-titled seven-inch on Lookout Records, and our full-length LP that came out on Ebullition. *Mi Cuerpo Es Mío* was an Allied release. We chose Allied because of our ties, mostly through Karin, with John Yates, who ran Allied, and because we had decided that we would not be owned by any one particular record label, especially since like the punk scene itself the punk record labels were run by men. We were of course grateful for these particular men, but we didn't want any of them to feel any kind of ownership over us, our music, or our message. I remember Karin framing our approach that way, and it made sense to me after experiencing a great deal of embarrassment from comments made during the release of the Kamala and the Karnivores seven-inch, *Girl Band*, which came out in 1989 when I was still dating founding partner of Lookout Records David Hayes. Back then a few people actually said that Kamala and Karnivores only got to make our record on Lookout because I was dating David, but it turns out that *Girl Band* was just a really good record after all. And it had a brilliant cover concept inspired by *Superstar: The Karen Carpenter Story*, a movie that Ivy and I had seen and loved. On the cover of *Girl Band*, each member of Kamala and the Karnivores is depicted with Barbie dolls, as has had been done in the movie. We even found a brown-skinned Barbie for my doll and an Asian Barbie for Lynda who played guitar.

During my days entrenched in the scene, I never tried to pass for white, but my nickname was Todd and people didn't always go by their last names. Familial ties were less important than what band you were in, zine you wrote, or city you were from, and a lot of us were from divorced or dysfunctional families anyway. If you were in a band, you went by your first name and your last name was the name your band: Todd

Spitboy, Adrienne Spitboy, and so on. Before Spitboy, people called me Todd Bitch Fight.

Although I looked quite different from the rest of the Spitboy, my ethnicity didn't often come up in conversation, not in the Bay Area. In the 1990s, people were still trying to be colorblind, to not see race, or to pretend not to see it, as the case may be. It wasn't polite to talk about race, and so I didn't really talk about it, but one conversation sticks out in my mind:

"What's your last name?"

We had just played a show and a friend of Karin's had come to see us play.

"Gonzales," I said. It was an unusual question.

"Your last name is Gonzales? Are you, um, Mexican?"

"Yeah, I am," I said.

This was sort of nice—most people usually said, "What are you?"

"How come I didn't know that before?"

"I don't know."

"That's so weird. I'm sorry," said Karin's friend who was blonde and pretty normal-looking, the kind of girl one might assume was sheltered by privilege.

"What do you mean?"

"It seems like I should have known that before. I've seen you play and Spitboy, you know, you're a punk band. I never thought about you all being anything other than that."

"Oh, yeah," I said.

"I feel bad." She reached out and touched my knee.

I didn't know what to say.

"Identity is so important, and I didn't even see it, see you. I just saw Spitboy."

"I don't think that's uncommon," I said, "It's easier just to see the short hair and clothes I guess."

"Well, I'm not going to do that again," she said, "It's not right."

After so many years of race/class ridicule that I endured growing up in Tuolumne, fitting in was important to me, but fitting into the punk scene the way I did then created a whole other problem. In conforming to the nonconformist punk ways, adhering, mostly, to the punk uniform, I had lost something along the way, and I began to experience rumblings of discontent that I didn't quite understand. I secretly listened to Linda Ronstadt's *Canciones de Mi Padre* and sang along, holding long sad notes to words that, like Ronstadt, I only vaguely understood. I knew that my identity was the root of my confusion and discontent, so I began taking Spanish classes at a local community college when I could fit them in after work.

Learning to speak Spanish had been a lifelong dream. As a child, someone had given me a red hardcover Spanish/English dictionary, and naively I thought if I read it every night before bed that I would become bilingual like the rest of my family in East LA. Later, living in the Bay Area and not being able to speak Spanish began messing with my head, made me feel inadequate, like a phony. I sometimes avoided going to the Mission District in San Francisco because while I was working super hard to fit into the punk scene, playing in bands, going to shows, and volunteering at Blacklist, and not always feeling totally accepted or understood, I felt really out of place in the Mission where it seemed like everyone spoke to me in Spanish and looked baffled when I couldn't respond. Learning to speak my family's language, even the little that I was able to speak after only a couple of semesters of college Spanish, provided some relief and helped me to come out as a person of color in the punk scene.

I didn't say all of this out loud when I suggested *Mi Cuerpo Es Mío* as the title for what would become our last release with Paula in the band because I still didn't really have words to express all that was going on inside me at twenty-five. Later, when I did have the words, they often came out wrong, clumsy, angry, abrasive, and alienating, especially in those last days of Instant Girl, but I suppose this was part of my process.

Everyone in the band liked the phrase "mi cuerpo es mío" because of its strength in sound and content and because it summed up all that we were about. The syntactical alignment of the masculine ending noun "cuerpo" and pronoun "mío" is what creates the strength in the line and is an aspect of the Spanish language that makes it particularly euphonious and easy to create rhyme. It was also a concept of the language that I understood particularly well, and I when I learned it, I was drawn to the way it created emphasis.

Still, the main reason that I suggested "mi cuerpo es mío" as the title of the seven-inch was to acknowledge an aspect of my membership in the band that I felt was missing, an aspect of myself that I felt unable to or insecure about expressing. Blame the scene, blame Tuolumne, blame America. It could have been any number of those things. Probably all of them together were to blame for my *locura*, for my schizophrenic or closeted identity.

I hadn't been at all sure that the Spitwomen would want to name our record "My Body Is Mine" in Spanish, but they did, and that felt good, but being criticized by a riot grrrl was a huge blow. It really pissed me off.

Like a lot of people, my first reaction to anything upsetting back then was anger. Anger is a good mask for sadness, so I didn't understand right away that I wasn't really mad that some riot grrrl, keen on accusing people of cultural appropriation but who couldn't recognize a person of color when she was staring one in the face, had attacked the band. I was hurt, hurt because people didn't really see me and that I had let it happen. People in the scene did not see me, who I really was at the core, the face and body through which I experienced the world. At shows, I did not register as a Xicana. I was just the drummer of Spitboy, and for some reason I couldn't be both.

Kurt Cobain Is Dead

I had seen Nirvana play on the eve of 1993 at the Oakland Coliseum. Jason, my Little Rock boyfriend, had a connection, so went backstage and watched the show from the stage itself on a row of bleachers set up for the VIP guests. We knew better than to try to speak to the moody Kurt Cobain, but we drank free beer, played pinball, and hung around friends in Green Day and Monsula, the band Jason was in at the time.

Punk rockers weren't supposed to like mainstream music, but everyone I knew liked Nirvana, and Spitboy loved Liz Phair. Both Nirvana and Liz Phair were cut from the same cloth, only Nirvana was on a major label, and Phair was on Matador, a swanky independent label, so we always felt like we lost some punk points when we put on those CDs on the battery-operated boom box. But we did it anyway, choosing to somewhat ignore the major-label controversy, choosing to allow our taste in music to move forward with the times.

Paula had already left the band, having had trouble off and on with wrist pain and struggling with missing Pete the Roadie, with whom she was now in a very serious relationship. It was hard for me to see Paula go. It felt like a huge loss, but there was little tension around her leaving since it was something that she had told us she was thinking about doing while we were on tour in Europe, and we knew that she had doubts over the years about her bass playing, worrying that she didn't play as well as the rest of us. While none of that mattered to me at all, I didn't really understand why anyone would want to leave a thriving band. But I did understand Paula's struggle with self-doubt and that she was thinking seriously about moving to England to be with Pete. I had never ever seen anyone before, or maybe since, in love with someone the way that she was, and still is, with Pete.

Paula wasn't out of the band long at all when Adrienne introduced us to Dominique. They met through some younger female scenesters, who hung around at the famous Green Day house where the video for "Longview" was filmed, across the street from Whole Foods in Berkeley where Adrienne worked at the time. With Paula out of the band, Adrienne bought a newer model van, which we needed now that we no longer had a bass player/mechanic in the band. Our new bass player, Dominique, a classically trained cellist, was a great musician. She was also studying architecture, so she designed and helped build our new van's loft. We had lost a mechanic but gained an architect. Dominique was younger than the rest of us, quirky in all the right ways, always nibbling on a bar of dark chocolate, which she kept close by in her messenger bag. She brought a fresh energy to the band. And with Dominique, our songwriting got more complex, though not necessarily better. When Adrienne left the band and Karin, Dominique, and I transformed into Instant Girl, we went back to straight-forward four-four punk beats; these songs were punctuated by crisp stops and starts and lots of crashing cymbals.

On our first US tour with Dominique, we played a string of shows with Citizen Fish, with whom we had toured in England a couple of years earlier when Paula was still in the band. Both Pete and Paula were on the road with Citizen Fish. Being all together, touring with our new bass player and with our old bass player on the road crew of another band, put both Paula and Dominique in a strange position. But being women who did not wish to perpetuate catty, competitive stereotypes of women, everyone was determined to rise above it. I knew it was going to be hard for Paula to watch Dominique play her old songs, songs she wrote the bass lines for, and to see Dominique play new songs that Paula would never play. Still, I saw Paula nodding her head as we played and Pete the Roadie stood just offstage ready to help if anything went wrong with my drum kit. To this day, Paula asks after Dominique and Dominique asks after Paula, which I can only attribute to the success of our commitment to make that transition without too much tension, or drama, and to do it with love and for love, too.

Dominique's entrance into the band was marked by a time of great change in the punk scene. We were getting a little older, punk was becoming mainstream, and some punks were less afraid to admit that they didn't only listen to punk music. Spitboy must have listened to *Exile in Guyville* by Liz Phair at least a hundred times while on the four-week spring 1993 tour. I'd often sit in front while Dominique drove the van and we'd sing to "Divorce Song" or "Fuck and Run," driving down the interstate to our next show, "I woke up alarmed/I didn't know where I was at first/Just that I woke up in your arms." I loved sitting in the passenger seat of the van where it felt like I could see the whole world out the large windshield, singing in my best voice, the midday sun shining all over me. Punk going mainstream made getting pulled over by police officers a bit less fraught, and we were women, mostly white women, so we appeared to pose a very little threat.

More than halfway to the East Coast, we got pulled over by a highway patrol one night after a show, and after Dominique, whose driving we all worried a bit about, had swerved on the narrow freeway in high winds. She went a little pale, looking in the rearview mirror, police lights flashing, a cop with a gun approaching the van.

"I stopped you because you were swerving around back there on the highway," said the red-faced officer now at our window.

"Sorry about that, officer."

I watched the exchange from the back seat where I sat with Karin. Adrienne was in the loft, and our roadie, Phyllis, was in the passenger seat.

"Identification?"

"No, officer, I haven't taken any medication, just this." Dominique rummaged around in her messenger bag, old receipts and chocolate wrappers falling onto the floor, and to our horror she produced a bottle of ibuprofen, which she held up for the cop to see.

"No, Ma'am, I asked to see your identification."

Phyllis stifled what would normally be a loud guffaw, and Karin beside me and Adrienne in the loft stayed quiet, perhaps hoping not to be seen.

The cop swept his Maglite inside the van, shining it over each of us, probably making a mental note of how many of us there were.

"Where are you ladies headed tonight?"

"We're in a band, sir," Dominique responded.

"A band, eh?" He lifted his flashlight again, shining it on Adrienne with her wild hair.

"That one there is the singer, ain't she?"

Dominique nodded her head. "Yes, sir, that's Adrienne, she's the singer."

"I knew it," he said, "The wild-looking one is always the singer." He nodded his head and smiled, looking pleased with himself, then went back to his car to run the license and registration information.

While she seemed young and mostly carefree, I hadn't realized that Dominique worried a lot on this tour about roadie Phyllis (perhaps as much as we fretted about her driving the van, as she hadn't had a lot of experience with that). Phyllis had begged Dominique to be able come on the tour, making the case that she played drums, too, (in the Tourettes) and that she could be a big help tearing down my drums and moving the other equipment. While we all ran in similar circles in the Bay Area punk scene, Phyllis was considerably younger than the rest of us, only sixteen, and Dominique had promised her mom that nothing would happen to her. Nothing did, but not for the lack of trying on Phyllis's part.

Dominique happened to be driving when we pulled up to Rutgers University for a show the day that Kurt Cobain died. We hadn't yet bought the *Nevermind* CD, though I had the LP at home. But we did stop somewhere to buy it shortly after, which sadly, once Kurt was dead, was less uncool. I guess Kurt may have been right to worry about how the band would be accepted after they signed, but none of it was as black-and-white in reality as it may have appeared.

In his memoir, *Nirvana: The True Story*, Everett True comments on the effect it had on Kurt Cobain and Nirvana, who felt shunned by the punk scene once they signed to Geffen Records, having members of Green Day, Monsula, and Spitboy accept free backstage passes: "All these punk kids from this notoriously holier-than-thou scene were psyched to be there. . . . What a coup it was to have all these ideological punk rockers going round saying how amazing the show was, despite having called them sell-outs." It was probably hard for Kurt to deal with things others said about him, feeling insecure and under the devastating effects of heroin. What he didn't realize is that for many of us who were friends with Green Day, and had been for years, our feelings about selling out weren't as cut-and-dried as he thought. Some of us chose not to use the S word, as many of us felt we had grown up together.

On April 8, 1994, the day the news of Cobain's suicide broke, Dominique was driving and Phyllis was in the passenger seat when we pulled up to the dining hall where we'd play on the Rutgers campus. We parked in a small parking lot by a dumpster as we'd been instructed to do when we called ahead on a payphone. A couple of young guys, students, were there as Dominique navigated the van into the narrow back lot off the kitchen. One of the young men came sprinting over to the van, to the driver-side window before Dominique could even stop the van or open the door to get out.

"Did you hear? Did you hear the news? Kurt Cobain is dead!"

We were stunned. We hadn't heard the news. Touring in the days before cell phones and widespread use of the internet was isolating, though we didn't really see it that way because we had Liz Phair, travel Scrabble, our books, and each other. While driving all day, we had been no doubt chatting about the show the night before, singing along to *Exile in Guyville* or CDs by some of our other favorite bands like Unwound and Jawbreaker, driving from some other state when the news broke.

"What?" Dominique said, looking back at the rest of us to make sure we heard what she heard. Somehow we all knew, being younger, that she would take it harder than the rest of us. The rest of us had already suffered many other losses.

"Suicide. They think he shot himself," our Rutgers tour contact said as soon as Dominique put the van in park and opened the door to get out.

I moved over to sit on the corner of the passenger seat with Phyllis as Dominique got out of the van. I looked out at the trees on the Rutgers campus, over toward the covered dumpster we had parked alongside, and back to Adrienne and Karin, who were both sitting on the bench seat in the back. We were all unusually quiet as we let the news sink in.

As I looked out into the trees on the Rutgers campus, I wondered how we would play, but I knew we would, and I thought about my boyfriend back home, Jason, who was younger too and liked to watch TV alone, wondering how he must have felt sitting by himself on the couch when the news flashed up on the screen.

Our Favorite Assumptions

People assumed all sorts of things about Spitboy that weren't exactly true. People thought we were gay, and we weren't, even though 80 percent of the band had had sex with at least one other woman. People assumed we were all vegan, and Karin was, Adrienne was sometimes, and Dominique who joined later was, but Paula and I were not. And some people thought that we were crusty punks, but that was just because Adrienne had what looked like dreadlocks but was really just lace tied in her hair.

The two things people thought that surprised us the most were that we were mean and angry or wild partiers. Everywhere we went on our first full US tour, the people we met along the way—fans, tour contacts, and members of other bands—often made the same comment.

"You guys are sooooo nice," to which we at first responded by saying thank you, unsure of what else to say. Were we really that nice?

And it wasn't only other women who felt compelled to comment on our niceness. Men said it, too. It wasn't until about midway through the tour that we thought to ask what that meant.

"People have been saying that wherever we go," Karin said.

We were chatting with the woman whose house we were staying at after the show.

"Yeah, why do you think that is?" Paula asked.

"Well," she started off slowly, choosing her words carefully, "I just didn't think you'd all be so nice."

"Why wouldn't we be?" Karin asked.

"Yeah, we're staying at your house. We wouldn't be mean, would we?" I added.

"Well, it's just that, well, your music, your songs . . . You seem so angry."

Adrienne smiled wide and let out a loud laugh.

"I guess I expected you all to be real serious offstage, too, but it's like the opposite. You're all so nice and funny and smiling most of the time." She had gained confidence now explaining what she meant.

I remember being scared at fourteen, going to punk shows in San Francisco, and not just because I was from a small town. The older punk kids seemed so angry and tough, and there was a lot of violence and drunk punks at shows at the Farm or the Mab. It was like some of the punks who went to see Dead Kennedys took songs like "Too Drunk to Fuck" literally. Since Spitboy was not a party band, and since we were women, I hadn't imagined that anyone would be intimidated by us in this way. I never thought that anyone would expect us to be stomping-around-angry, the way we sometimes appeared to be onstage. I suppose it was a combination of how we sounded and looked, combined with stereotypes about angry feminists.

It may have been the anarcho-crusty punk look that Adrienne rocked (or that people saw) that was responsible for some of these stereotypes given that singers and how they look come to represent just about any band. But sometimes I just blamed Econochrist. Regardless of singer Ben Sizemore's straight edge, bands like Econochrist had somewhat cemented the assumption that hardcore applied to partying too. Perhaps it was stories about Jon Sumrall and Mike Scott getting wasted before a show and still being able to play that caused people to think we'd want to stay up all night drinking with them, but no one in Spitboy liked to play intoxicated and none of us were heavy drinkers, even though I did overdo it on occasion at home. In fact, we thought it was cliché for bands to get wasted before a show, onstage, or as soon as they were finished. It was too rock-n-roll and not in-the-moment enough for us. We were a punk band with a message, so drinking before a show became against Spitboy code, not to mention dangerous. My inner thighs were already covered in bruises from accidently hitting them all the time with the butts of my sticks, and I had learned my lesson about playing drunk with my first band Bitch Fight. We were at a party, and I was playing after drinking a couple of Old Milwaukees, and I hit myself in the mouth with a Vick Firth Classic Rock stick. I could have lost a tooth.

On tour (especially in Europe), Spitboy may have had one glass of wine with dinner before a late show, but we usually only drank after we played, and then not very much because we were too tired already, or didn't want to be tired or hungover for the long drive the next day.

In Europe, Pete, Nolde, and Eric, our road crew, drank more than we did, Nolde and Eric taking turns, depending on who was driving, and we'd join them sometimes, but only after we'd played. Pete the Roadie learned our preferences for drinking early in the tour—what, when, and how much—and he'd often offer to get me a beer once all the drums were torn down and put aside.

"Beer, drummer?" he'd say.

Sometimes he'd just bring me one, and when he did this I'd drink it, even if I really didn't want to, surprised to be waited on or considered in this way. Even though Pete was out of his head in love with Paula, he was good company. He'd sit with me at a table or at the bar while I drank my beer, offering me cigarettes or a drag off his because I fancied myself a nonsmoker.

"You want to smoke some hash?" Nolde asked me one night outside a club after a show in Germany.

"Hash? Oh, I don't know," I said. I was sitting inside the van, and Nolde was standing outside in front of me with the door open. Pete was there, too.

Nolde was a tall, strapping German with super long legs and bleached blond hair. He was handsome in a rugged Nordic way, but I had a boyfriend.

"You ever smoke hash, drummer?" Pete asked.

"Maybe, a long time ago," I said, pretty sure I hadn't. They all knew that I did not smoke anything but an occasional cigarette. Everyone in Spitboy had tried marijuana in her teens, but none of us smoked it. In terms of potency, hash seemed like a step up, and I wasn't so sure I could handle it. On the other hand, I was in Europe, and there was probably no better time to try something new.

"Do you smoke it just like that?" I asked looking at the oily-looking black nub that Nolde held sitting on a piece of foil.

"The best way to do it is to put a little of it in some tobacco. Make a cigarette," Pete said, knowing my weakness for cigarettes.

I laughed and shook my head.

"Okay, let's try it."

Eric, who always rolled his own cigarettes, rolled one for us, adding in some hash, not too much, at my urging, and we got in the van and smoke it. The hash made me giggle and it made me feel like kissing Nolde, which I did not do because of the boyfriend back home. He stretched out next to me on the loft in the back of the van as Eric drove us to our lodging for the night. I giggled the whole way there, trying to explain to Nolde what was so funny about the name of my sleeping bag—the Slumberjack.

"Slumberjack, it's a play on words." I tried to keep a straight face and not laugh.

He smiled, but I knew he didn't get it.

"Slumber is another name for sleep in English."

"Yes, I've heard this word," he said, looking up at me from a propped arm.

I started giggling again, hoping he didn't think that I was laughing at him, once again struck by how just about everyone else we came across on tour spoke English and that was pretty much all we could speak.

"But that's not what makes it funny," I continued.

"It rhymes with the word 'lumber,' and a lumberjack is a guy who cuts big logs of wood."

I was laughing now, and so was Karin, because it really was absurd to be explaining any of this at all.

Nolde stretched out looking at me, his long legs reaching all the way out, touching the wall of the van. He still didn't get it.

"Do you know Paul Bunyan? He's a lumberjack from a children's story. He has a blue ox."

"What is this? A blue ox?"

Karin, Jon, and I were all laughing now. It took a second to catch my breath I was laughing so hard.

"The blue ox, it's not real," I choked, tears streaming down my face.

* * *

Two years later, on our Pacific Rim tour of New Zealand, Australia, and Japan, Spitboy discovered the joys of Scrabble. Karin bought a travel Scrabble set, the kind that folds up and has tiny, easy-to-lose tiles that snap in place, allowing the board to be stored away and the game resumed after the next show. In New Zealand, the first country on the tour, we rode in rented van, a Rent-a-Dent, driven by Ross, who Karin had collaborated with to book the tour. A longtime employee of Mordam records, Karin handled their overseas sales and had many contacts, making it possible to for a band like Spitboy to tour like we did. New Zealand's Ross had high cheekbones, a floppy mohawk, and wore bondage pants, but he smiled too much to pull off a classic English punk look, never sneering or flipping the bird. We were all in love with him as soon as we met him at the airport, where he picked us up. The van didn't seem to have a dent on it and in fact had enough space in the way back where someone Dominique's height could lie down and sleep, which she did a lot, rising up with her sweatshirt hood still on, eyes blinking from the bright sun, that we nicknamed her Nessie after the Loch Ness Monster.

Ross was excited to meet us and to introduce us to his friends in Auckland and to take us to see some sights, like the harbor, an indoor bathhouse, and faroff snow-covered mountains. He assured us that even though we were playing all-ages shows that there'd be time to party afterward, but we were more interested in what we were going to eat and where we were going to sleep. Karin, Dominique, and our roadie/photographer Karoline Collins were all vegan and would read Lonely Planet guides in advance of each new country for tips on restaurants. Karoline had toured the Pacific Rim, and she also had several recommendations. A café with vegetarian/vegan sausage sandwiches particularly stands out in my memory.

Once Dominique arrived on a different flight (she flew for free since her dad, Captain Bob, was a pilot for American Airlines), and once I recovered a bit from terrible vertigo and jetlag, we played in Auckland, and then set off with Ross for five or six more shows and a couple of very long drives. On these long drives, we became consumed by our Scrabble games. Four people can play the board game, and sometimes all of Spitboy would play, or Karoline would play with Karin, Dominique, and me. Adrienne often felt compelled to copilot, sitting with Ross up front in the van, to keep him company. Karin usually won at Scrabble because she had the biggest vocabulary and the best offensive and defensive strategies, and I usually lost. Losing never dampened my spirits for the game, or for the chance to pull out the dictionary that Karin also brought for challenging the validity of a word or correct spelling. We weren't cutthroat players, but we did play by the rules, consulting the slim folded sheet of paper that came with the game whenever we needed to. And when one of us was taking a long time on a turn, the others would simply plan the next turn, hoping our desired spot on the board wasn't used, watch the sights out the window as they rolled by, or even taking out a book. I had bought a book of short stories written by Maori authors in Auckland, and I undoubtedly had another book from home by some Latina author in my bag.

After being our driver and tour manager for a couple of days, Ross realized that we weren't big partiers, and he made a comment to that end that made us all squeal and love him even more. We were getting back into the van after stopping to stretch our legs at a rest area with a picnic bench where we snacked on hunks of soft baguettes. As soon as we got into the van, before we even got moving, Karin pulled out the Scrabble board and asked whose turn it was. This was one of our biggest problems with Scrabble: when we had to stop midgame and resume, we could hardly ever remember who was next.

"I remember Dominique spelled 'joe,'" I said.

"But someone went after me." She was looking at the board.

"Here, let me see the score sheet," said Karoline.

Ross, who had been fiddling with something on the driver's side door, turned around. "You guys are like a bunch of old ladies," he said with a big smile.

We all looked up. Karin had the Scrabble board open on her lap.

"I wasn't expecting this at all. When I booked Spitboy, I was think-ing we'd be raging all night long, having wild parties, and getting really wasted."

"Really? You thought that?" Karin said. Karin always smiled.

We had grown fond of hearing what people thought we might be like, what strange assumptions people had about female hardcore-play-ing feminists, but maybe it was weird that we played so much Scrabble.

"No sex, drugs, and rock and roll for this lot," someone said.

"Really," Ross said. "My grandmother plays Scrabble."

I rather liked being compared to Ross's grandmother, an old woman who liked words and social time with her friends, and I liked that once again Spitboy was defying stereotypes and preconceived notions about who we were, what we did, and how we did it.

Homesickness Cure

On all of Spitboy's tours—the ten-day tour, the two US tours, six weeks in Europe, and the Pacific Rim tour—I only kissed two people. There were no strict unwritten rules about dating or sleeping around in the Bay Area punk scene, and if there had been, I wouldn't have followed them anyway, but touring was different. I felt different about it. Even though punk rock bands don't attract groupies in the traditional sense, there are hangers on, people who find you a lot more interesting just because you are in a band, and that set me on edge. Spitboy also feared date rape.

Regular people in regular bands, usually men, did sleep around on tour, and even though I never did it, I could understand why. Even though it sounds cliché, it gets lonely on the road. While together and united as a band, individually, you are overwhelmed by each new place where you are a novelty and not exactly a person. Since I was what people still called a minority in both the punk scene and in America, and maybe because I was still young, I didn't feel like I quite fit in anywhere. Perhaps I thought being in a band, being a part of the scene in this central way would fix that feeling, but it never did, so the loneliness of tour may have bothered me more than it did anyone else. I was certainly the member of Spitboy most often found sitting in the van alone, reading a book or writing in her journal. To find solace at the end of our European tour, having read all the books I had brought with me, I read a book Adrienne had with her, a Stephen King novel, *Gerald's Game*, even though I don't like Stephen King novels. I finished it just before I had to go onstage at our last show in Belgium. I do not, however, recommend a book about a woman stuck alone in a cabin, handcuffed to a bed after accidentally killing her husband, who got too rough with her during what had started off as consensual bondage sex, to ward off feelings of loneliness and alienation.

"Couldn't you live here?" Karin would gush every time we looked out over a city on a body of water during the Pacific Rim tour.

From the top of a hill looking over the bay in Auckland, from a boat on Sydney Harbour.

"Couldn't you live here? I could. I could live here."

"I could," Dominique would say when the view was particularly beautiful.

I'd stay quiet because I knew they wouldn't want to hear my answer. I had recently realized that my feelings of alienation from the punk scene stemmed from my somewhat closeted ethnic identity, and I didn't think they'd understand.

I hadn't realized how accustomed I was to living in the Bay Area, always being around Latinos, and street names and cities named in Spanish, until Karin asked this question. Then I met Sabrina.

Even though I was basically single, in an open relationship during the Pacific Rim tour, I chose to be celibate as I had on all the other tours, with only one minor lapse. Sabrina was a Latina, and a woman.

In my mind, women were safe; there was less literal risk involved, and I had gotten to know Sabrina a bit because she came to a few of our shows, traveling with friends to see us. One night in our van, we sat side by side, our thighs touching, my heart pounding the whole ride. Adrienne, Karin, and Dominique pretended not to notice each time we looked at one another, little fluttery glances that made Sabrina blush and lower her head each time she caught my eye. When we got to the venue, maybe it was in Melbourne, I loaded in my equipment, the snare drum in the hard shell case, the twenty-five-pound bag of cymbals, and my case of sticks as fast as I could. I suffered through a boring soundcheck then snuck off to find Sabrina hanging around the front of the stage.

"You want to go for a walk?" I said.

"Yeah." She lowered eyes and smiled.

I grabbed her by the arm and pulled her toward the closest door. I was older and more experienced. The sun had already set, but we found our way to the back of the venue by street lamp, and weak in the knees we sat down on a curb. She told me about her family and life in Sydney. She had creamy olive skin and a furry hat. She was Australian by birth but ethnically Argentinian. I have no idea what her family was doing in Australia, but I was glad she was there, and when I didn't feel like talking anymore I leaned in and kissed her on the mouth, and she leaned into me, her curves soft on my tight drummer's body.

Growing up in a mini-punk scene in Tuolumne in which there were only about twelve of us at any one time, I was very insecure about how I looked. It was cooler to have narrow bony shoulders and pale skin. It wasn't uncommon for the guys to say I was pretty but that my skin was too dark. Having matured some and grown into my identity a bit, I no longer felt shame about being Mexican or having a strong boxy frame, but that experience made me wary, especially on tour. That people found me interesting or attractive just because I was in a band was the opposite of anything I had ever experienced before. It caused me to form my own rule. I would not sleep with anyone on tour even if I were single. I didn't want to be hugged by someone I didn't know, and I certainly wasn't going to have sex with someone I didn't know because I knew that if I did, it would have only happened because I was in a band, because I was the drummer of Spitboy.

Soundchecks, Long Sets, and Lesbians

ouring can sometimes make you feel like you're in a parallel universe. The settings are different, the rules change, and bands must rely on the knowledge and guidance of representatives from each new galaxy. Sometimes the rules changed due to cultural ignorance or language barriers, like they did for me in France where I clung to Karin, who spoke the language, afraid to commit some kind of terrible French faux pas, or for Adrienne, who much later in Japan accidently tromped all over our hosts' tatami mats in her heavy leather boots after the rest of us had removed our shoes at the door.

In the United States, Spitboy never played longer than thirty-minutes, played all-ages shows, and only charged five dollars per T-shirt. It was so hard to keep the T-shirt prices down that we not only screened them ourselves, but we spent a lot of time in thrift stores buying used T-shirts to screen-print on. We realized, though, that buying our shirts in thrift stores had additional benefits. Those Beefy-T's that we bought to screen on initially were boxy, too hot to play in, and unflattering on women. In thrift stores we found quarter-length sleep baseball T's, scoop-neck cap-sleeve T's, and feminine cuts, and worn in, but not worn out butch-cut T-shirts that butch women and men might be more likely to buy. Before flying to Japan, however, we were told that no one would buy used shirts and that we had to sell them for at least ten dollars.

Having shirts made sure was easier than screening our own T-shirts when we ran out on tour, where we'd have to find time and a place to make more. We had to make more after a show that I barely remember in New Orleans because I had been almost too sick to play in the first place. After the show, I slept in the van on some street somewhere while the rest of the band walked the French Quarter and had drinks before going back to stay with the woman, Shannon, who helped organize our show. She lived with her parents outside of the city somewhere, and her dad, a balding man with a belly, kindly made sure that we got those shirts made before we got back on the road for our next show.

The DIY T-shirt screen-printing process takes many steps. Each shirt must be screened individually, and to do it quickly on the road without a professional setup and a utility sink takes at least three people. You need two people to screen the image on the shirt, one to hold the screen and another to pull the ink across the screen onto the shirt. The third person is needed to take the freshly screened shirt to hang on a clothesline or any semi-clean flat surface to dry. A fourth person pulls an unprinted T-shirt out of the box and places it on the flat screening surface. Usually a table covered in layers of newspaper is ideal because anyone at the screen-printing table is bound to get ink on her hands and because the more T-shirts you make, the clothesline or other flat surfaces used for drying can get really far away. Once the ink dries on each shirt, which can take quite a long time but only an hour or two when put out to dry in the hot summer sun, the T-shirts must be put in a dryer on high heat to set the ink. This was often my job, putting the shirts on the line, transferring from the line to the dryer and taking them back out again because I made too much of a mess with the ink. I do remember standing in the hot New Orleans sun in Shannon's yard, dry weeds beneath my feet, pinning T-shirts to her clothesline, a row of nippled women flapping in the breeze at only ten or so in the morning.

Because we always had at least a three- or four-hour drive between shows, and often longer, we had to get up early in the morning to get the T-shirts printed, dried, folded, and put away in time. Shannon's dad was eager to help, offering his kitchen table as the printing station, taking a turn at each step in the process.

"It didn't come out right," he said, after printing his first shirt, the nipple on the woman on the logo staring back up at him. "Let me try again."

He gave up printing the T-shirts fairly quickly because it does take quite a bit of practice to get a good print, but I do have a photo of him sitting cross-legged, wearing shorts and socks, on his living room floor near his easy chair folding a Spitboy shirt, a pile of shirts beside him.

In Europe, T-shirts weren't an issue, but we were told we had to play longer sets and do soundchecks. I hated soundchecks. Soundchecks made me feel like a fake. When soundchecking, you don't play your best, or your hardest; you don't even play a full song. It's an all-out going through the motions to get the all the levels right. The drums can't be allowed to drown out the guitar and bass, and nothing should drown out the vocals. Spitboy had four vocal mics, and those had to be checked too. Then we had to check the levels of the vocals in the monitors. In small halls or clubs, often not meant for live music, soundchecks felt like an exercise in futility because one, or often all of us, could not hear what we needed to during the majority of the show, even when we had been able to hear ourselves during the soundcheck. Sound engineers have a tough job, and they probably often feel disliked by musicians. I've seen a lot of musicians bark into the mics at sound engineers, demanding more vocals in the monitor, or less guitar.

The headlining acts usually got to soundcheck first. I suppose the reason for this is to give the headlining act the most time to relax before the show, but this means arriving to venues early, and hoping that the sound engineer isn't just trying to memorize your levels but is actually marking them with a grease pencil on tape on the soundboard. Sound engineers don't tell musicians how to do their jobs and musicians don't usually tell engineers how to do theirs, so I'll never really know, but there were a few times when it felt like what we did during the soundcheck had little to do with the result of the sound on the stage. I tried not to ever get too frustrated when this happened because, after all, it was a punk show. Still I hated soundchecking, probably because soundchecking drums takes a lot longer than guitar, bass, or vocals. Usually, I'd sit alone onstage, listening for the engineer's voice over a microphone, waiting to be told what to do.

"Bass drum." Engineers always started with the bass drum.

I'd hit the bass drum, thunk, thunk, thunk, thunk, usually four times, staring down at the sound booth, usually straight ahead of me at the opposite end of the venue as the stage, wishing I could see the person speaking to me.

"Snare."

Whack, whack, whack. Pause. Whack, whack, whack.

"Left tom."

Thud, thud, thud.

"Okay, right."

Thud, thud, thud.

It always got so boring that I'd start to wonder what the others were doing, where they were, what they were talking about, and when I was feeling insecure, if they were talking about me.

"Floor tom."

Thunk, thunk, thunk. Pause. Thunk, thunk, thunk.

"All together."

I loved when the sound guy said "all together" because that's when I actually got to play, even if just for a few seconds. Doon, dat, doo, doo, doo, dat. At this point the rest of the band would drift in, put on their instruments, and I'd have to sit there, while the engineer went through the same routine with the guitar, the bass, guitar, then Adrienne's mic, mine, and the other two backup mics. When we finally got to play a song, one in which all the vocal mics were put to use, the engineer would signal for us to stop once we were halfway through. No one likes being told to stop playing one of her songs halfway through, especially when she's finally just started feeling it.

Having to soundcheck early, often a few hours from the start time of the show, always put an early end to sightseeing, not that there was much time for that in our hectic schedule of twenty-eight shows in thirty-one days. Arriving in the nick of time for soundcheck at a youth center show in Germany, I sat behind the drums wondering where the rest of the Spitwomen were. There I finally admitted to myself how much I hated this seemingly futile requirement. My mind wandered to the swing set on the youth center grounds. We had parked in a lot near a small playground, and when I saw it I wanted to stop and sit down on it and have a relaxing swing alone, but we were already almost late and we didn't want to anger the sound engineer or be one of those bands that just did whatever they wanted.

Back home in the United States, Spitboy only ever played thirty-minute sets. Since our aim was not to be rock stars wanking away onstage, and since we had an important but loud message to deliver, we decided that it would be best to get onstage and deliver that message for thirty minutes and get off, hopefully leaving the crowd wanting more. When we got to England, we were promptly and gently told by Pete the Roadie and Citizen Fish that in England and Europe, the crowd would expect more. The crowds would feel slighted if we came all that way to play and only played a thirty-minute set. We understood, even if in the United States no one really cared how long you played and most clubs didn't have a good enough sound system or engineer to require a soundcheck. Bands in the United States were often instructed to play no longer than x number of minutes, to which Spitboy would always reply, "Oh, don't worry, we'll be finished way before that."

Perhaps one of the weirdest things to happen to Spitboy happened in Italy, where we also visited a beautiful natural hot springs early one morning before the sun came up after a long drive. The sulfur smell of rotten eggs from the springs was nearly overwhelming, but it had been at least three days since I showered, so unlike Adrienne and Paula, who refused to get up, Karin and I stripped nude with Nolde and Eric and we eased our tired bodies down into the super hot water, a stone bridge towering above us overhead and a lazy little river flowing along side. The night before bathing in the hot springs, we played in a squatted castle, Forte Prenestino, to five hundred people in Rome on Easter weekend. It was a show that began with a vegetarian/vegan meal in the castle dining hall and Paula and I having to be boosted on the stage by Nolde, Pete, and Erich because the stage was at least eight feet tall. It was so tall and wide that even though we decided not to push my drums all the way to the back, I still could barely see the crowd below when the rest of the Spitwomen, who were standing, towering over all the people on the floor below us.

In protest of Easter weekend, there had been a pro-choice rally at the Vatican, which culminated for many of the rally attendees at our show at the castle. Many of these women still carried their protest signs or had pro-choice messages scrawled on their T-shirts, so it surprised everyone when a voice rose up out of the crowd between songs. "I want to eat your pussy!"

Too far away, I didn't know what was going on. I just knew that Karin's guitar intro was the start of the next song, and I hadn't heard my cue.

Shocked by those words, Karin, Paula, and Adrienne, along with Pete, Nolde, and Erich, moved to the edge of the stage to see who had made the crass comment. Paula says that in a near total reverse of what might have happened in the United States, a crowd of petrified-looking guys at the foot of the stage parted like the seas, revealing a contingent of lesbians.

"I want to eat your pussy," one of them yelled again, waving her protest sign at Adrienne.

With that, Karin started the song, the rest of us joining in. I know that Pete, Nolde, and Erich breathed a collective sigh of relief that a real abusive heckling incident hadn't broken out, because they understood that Spitboy didn't like the idea of men fighting our battles for us or having to think of them as protection. We all knew, however, that having them on or near the stage, looking tough when necessary, was somewhat of a deterrent, just not for enthusiastic lesbians who had the hots for Adrienne. We had truly entered an alternate universe.

Viviendo Asperamente

I f Spitboy wasn't enough of an anomaly in punk, with four women playing straight-ahead hardcore, along came Los Crudos, four Latino guys from Chicago via Mexico and Uruguay, playing hardcore and singing in Spanish. I don't remember this, but Los Crudos singer Martín says that we met at a show they played in someone's backyard in Oakland. I do remember that I introduced myself to them as soon as they finished playing, all brown and glistening with sweat, and I offered them space to stay at my place, a punk house I lived in with Adrienne that was called the Maxi Pad because it was rented by women. Martín, José, Lenin, Joel, and I sat around the secondhand dining room table in mismatched chairs in a kitchen with a warped wooden floor and talked late into the night about what it was like to be on tour looking like them, a group of brown punk dudes all streaming out of a van all at once at service stations, short hair, long hair, pink hair, goatees, dirty jeans, and band T-shirts in Middle America. Martín teased Joel for asking that the band buy fabric softener for his clothes when they did laundry at a laundromat.

Nobody in the Bay Area punk scene expected a band like Los Crudos, least of all me. A Latino punk band in the United States, that was rare, even though there had been a few, like the Zeros from the LA area. It seemed all the Latino punks in bands were from the LA area. Sure, we had a few Latino punks in the East Bay scene, many who chose to pass or simply not acknowledge their ethnic identity and a couple who couldn't pass and didn't try. I could never pass, really, but I did vacillate between being quite vocal about my Xicanisma and trying to just fit in with everyone else because going it alone was too exhausting. Then Los Crudos appeared, singing about Latino issues in Spanish.

It was selfish, but I wanted them all to myself, offering them a place to stay and probably vegetarian beans and rice whenever they came to town.

Martín and I became instant friends. We were like long-lost relatives who stayed up all night talking and laughing, trying to make up for lost time. I cut his long hair short, lobbed off the ponytail in one jagged chop with dull scissors. I helped them screen T-shirts, drying them all around on the hedges in my yard, lent them my car to finish their tour when their van blew up, and went to every Crudos show I could.

The bond between Los Crudos and Spitboy quickly followed, as did the inevitable relationship with Crudos guitarist José. Until José, I had really only dated white guys in bands and I knew that there was something self-hating about it. My mom had forsaken Latino guys after my terror of a dad, but I had no such reason, so I allowed myself to believe that I didn't date Latino guys because there weren't very many around. My relationship with José came at a time when I began to feel more comfortable with my multiple identities: Spitboy drummer, feminist, Xicana. Still, I felt I had to keep my relationship with Jose as separate as possible from goings-on with the band, as Spitboy was uneasy mixing relationships and music and being defined by men.

In 1995, Spitboy and Los Crudos put out a split record, *Viviendo Asperamente*. Without access to the internet and e-mail, we decided the name of the record and shot around ideas for a cover image over the phone. The title was Martín's idea, as when we decided to make the record, the bands had agreed on two things straightaway: the title of the record would be in Spanish, and the cover image would be of a woman, a Latina. The title *Viviendo Aperamente*, or "roughly living," seemed to capture the content of the songs by both bands—Latino struggles and feminist struggles, living with such awareness was often abrasive, hard, rough. For me, after spending so many years feeling invisible, putting out a record with a cover image of a woman who looked like me felt like a personal victory. Still, there were other things that I had to consider carefully. In the booklet that came with the record, I thanked Los Crudos as a band and not individually by name, in order to keep things separate. I also knew, as much as I didn't want it to be true, that my relationship with José wouldn't last. Spitboy was still going strong, and I wasn't going to leave California, not even for the guitar player of Los Crudos. In the end, I wouldn't have to make any choice, one was made for me, but I did gain a better understanding of myself and learn to make more purposeful decisions about relationships.

People will say that Spitboy benefitted the most by putting out a record with what would become one of the most beloved hardcore bands in 1990s, and they'd be right, but there is more to it than that. In each other, Spitboy and Los Crudos found a band akin to the other, a band that was clear in message and resolute, charismatic, and endearing. It was a collaboration of message, sound, and mutual admiration.

Meanwhile, Los Crudos had screamed their way into the hearts of all good punks, blowing everyone away with their intensity and the way they told us all to fuck off by singing in their native Spanish. Those not fluent in Spanish, myself included, had to read translations of their lyrics if we wanted to know what their songs were about. And irony of all ironies, predominately white punk audiences from New York to Chicago, Detroit to Reno sang along in Spanish when Crudos played live. I couldn't quite believe it.

In July of 1998, two years after Spitboy disbanded and only a few months after I got married, something I had never planned on doing, I took my husband, Inés, to see Los Crudos. He had never been to a punk show before but, like everyone else, I knew he'd love Los Crudos. During the show, we stood at the side of the stage where I always watched bands at Gilman, and I watched the wide-eyed Inés, in his black beanie, watch them. He couldn't take his eyes off Martín as he performed, frantic, and guttural, and sincere. He nodded when Martín spoke about the damage done to Latino communities as a result of Proposition 187, and I was extra glad that I had brought him to the show, even though it meant a polite but awkward introduction to José and an embarrassing case of Latino mistaken identity.

After Crudos finished their set and put down their instruments, Inés and I stood near the stage. We were waiting to talk with Martín, to congratulate him on a great show. While we were standing around waiting for the mob around Martín to thin out, a young white punk guy came up and slapped Inés on the back.

"Great show, man." The young punk smiled wide and bobbed his head up and down.

Inés looked at me, then back at the young punk.

"You guys rocked," the guy said, seeming unsure if Inés had heard him.

Inés looked at me again.

I shrugged.

"Thanks," Inés said, because that's what Martín would have done. And he wanted the guy to go away.

I suppose this was progress. In just a few years, Latinos in the Bay Area punk scene went from being invisible to mistaken for members of Los Crudos.

Still, we went home that night and I didn't return to Gilman for another thirteen years. The punk scene's enthusiasm for Los Crudos was for me, and probably many others, an indirect form of personal validation. But the scene, like America, could only change so much so fast, and I didn't have the time or the patience to wait around and endure both.

Turning Japanese

Karin didn't ask any of us if we thought we could live in Japan the way she did all over New Zealand and Australia. But even for many of its peculiarities, I felt I could. Out of all the places we had traveled, I felt I had found my I-could-live-here place, though I would have never guessed that going in.

Before leaving the United States, we were informed that Japanese fans would not want to buy our T-shirts if we sold them too cheap. In preparation for the Pacific Rim tour, we had new shirts made for us by a professional company after we learned that Japanese fans would definitely not buy Spitboy gear handprinted on used thrift-store shirts. Not wanting used T-shirts we could sort of understand, but not buying them if we sold them for too little made no sense at all. Nevertheless, it was customary to sell merchandise, to offer items that extended the experience of seeing us, a punk band from the United States, and a female punk band at that, so we had T-shirts professionally made and shipped to Japan in advance of our arrival, knowing that we'd be able to make our money back since we had to charge more for T-shirts than we had ever charged or would ever charge back home.

Capitalist culture shock aside, I felt oddly at home in Japan. I had matured some in the two years since we had toured Europe, petrified by the language barrier in France and a fear of being judged by some haughty French person. Not being able to speak Japanese didn't bother me, even though I knew that some people there would understand English. If I went into a store alone without a translator, however, I would have to negotiate the whole transaction through a series of hand signals and nods and resist the urge to speak Spanish, the language that popped into my head each time. A friend, Ken Sanderson, a transplant from Auburn, Alabama, who had spent many years studying Japanese, gave Spitboy a couple of lessons on necessary phrases to learn for travel in Japan. He taught us phrases we'd need to know at the store (usually 24-Open) for rice balls and for riding the train (which we did at one point), as well as a few informal phrases that we'd want to use when we met the folks in the bands we'd be playing with: things like "yoroshiku" (nice to meet you) and "jaa ne," (see you later). I spent the whole plane ride between Australia and Japan studying my list of phrases, wanting to be prepared to speak for myself, or at least not be the ugliest American ever, but I wasn't prepared for what would happen when I got off the plane.

People usually noticed Adrienne everywhere Spitboy went. She always had the wildest hair and clothes, her hey-look-at-me personality matching the lead-singer type. Karin was noticeable for her great smile, and Dominique for being so tall, but when we got off the plane in Japan, suddenly I got all the attention.

"Pocahontas! Pocahontas!"

We didn't know what all the shouting was about, but when we turned toward the noise, we saw a Japanese teen shouting and pointing at me.

The Disney *Pocahontas* movie had come out that year and had apparently made quite an impression, because before I knew it, people all over the Kansai airport were turning to look in our direction, staring at me, pointing, and whispering to each other.

Before leaving Australia, where it had been winter, I read the weather reports for Japan, which had forecasted very hot days all week, and I had dressed accordingly and put my shoulder-length hair in braids, one on either side of my head.

Still, in spite of this awkward start, I acclimated to Japan better than the others. Old men in shops warmed to me faster than they did to the others, and I found a lot of the guys in punk bands attractive, as many of them had dark skin like mine, high cheek bones, small taut muscular frames, and almond-shaped eyes. You could also buy iced-coffee out of vending machines on the street. One particular brand, Boss Coffee, has a stylized logo of a man that looks like Ernest Hemingway smoking a pipe.

Our host, Naoki, guided us gently, explaining aspects of Japanese culture that he thought might be unfamiliar or startling to us, helping us avoid cultural faux pas, such as selling used T-shirts. Worried that we'd be thrown out of a traditional-style bathhouse for having tattoos, which were only worn then by the Yakuza, a Japanese crime syndicate, Naoki waited for us in the lobby. We found him pacing back and forth near the lobby fountain as we exited the women's side of the bathhouse all calm and relaxed. Naoki had organized our entire tour, which is quite difficult to do DIY-style in Japan without a company, a manager, or promoters, and he wanted us to see the sights, too, so he didn't try to talk us out of the bathhouse, and he offered to take us to the Sanrio amusement park not once but several times.

"Why does he keep asking if we want to go to see Hello Kitty?" Karin asked. We were all in his apartment in Ichikawa, just outside of Tokyo, in the room where we slept while there. We had a day off.

I didn't say anything because while I thought it was a bit strange, too, I also thought it was sort of sweet.

"Is it because we're women? Are we the kind of girls who like Hello Kitty?" she continued.

Adrienne, for whom Japan had been quite a culture shock, laughed. "I don't know."

Adrienne often laughed in times like these, rather than being critical or pretending to know the answer, she'd just laugh. It was a trait that I always admired.

"Maybe he's just trying to be hospitable," Dominique said.

I nodded, agreeing that it was odd that he had offered again to take us to the Sanrio Puroland when we had declined once already, and because I agreed with Dominique.

None of us knew, but the amusement park had only been open for a few years. It was still quite a new attraction, but we wanted to see *authentic* Japanese sights: tea houses, mount Fuji, sushi bars, and outdoor shopping centers like Asakusa where we could buy fans, kimonos, and Saki glasses. Even though I didn't say it, I would not have minded going to Sanrio Puroland, but just like when I was growing up in Tuolumne, I didn't have the money I'd need to buy unnecessary Hello Kitty items, things like notebooks, pens, coffee cups, or pencil purses. There had actually been a Sanrio store in Sonora, Tuolumne's county seat. The store only lasted a few months, closing before I could save the money to buy the plastic Hello Kitty head change purse that I saw and thought I'd have to have.

Even though I never admitted that I might have liked to visit Sanrio Puroland, I did probably gloat too often that I was enjoying Japan more than the others, and feeling less invisible. In Japan, a young woman, the drummer for An Apology Nature Arise and the human equivalent to Hello Kitty herself—small and cute and cartoonlike in dress—fell to her knees crying when she met me. An Apology Nature Arise was a band that we played with in Nagoya, and they wanted to meet us before the show. Naoki set up the meeting, which took place on the street outside of the club Huck Finn a few hours before the show. The band had a male and female singer, and a female drummer. The second we were introduced, the drummer, a tiny woman, shorter than me and much smaller-boned, with a pretty round face, a short skirt, and ribbons tied all in her hair, burst into tears, hugged me, and fell in a heap on the sidewalk.

Not knowing what else to do, I helped lift her off the ground. Between sobs she told me, through Naoki who translated, what an honor it was to meet me, another female drummer, and what an honor it was to meet Spitboy, their idols, women brave enough to spread our feminist message to the punk scene. I remember Adrienne, Karin, and Dominique looking at one another in shock as this woman cried in my arms. Naoki later explained that since the Japanese were typically a reserved people, when they did express emotion it was usually in quite a dramatic way. For a group of women who expressed their emotions all different ways at all different times, this explanation, which made sense, was still puzzling. The whole event left us all a bit quiet, and I sensed that I should not mention all the attention I was getting, and I dared not say anything like "I could live here" in the midst of growing tensions.

Japan, a non-Western nation, had tested us. And while our hosts made us feel welcome and attended to all our needs, we may not have been prepared or mature enough to understand or admit just how accustomed we were to Western ways, which accelerated already-growing rifts between us. Ebullition label owner Kent McClard, who joined us on the tour and was critical of everything everywhere we went, was no help. Trying to stay positive, I refused to admit to myself that I avoided riding in whichever car Kent or Adrienne were in (we did not have a van in Japan but instead traveled in a pack of three cars, all Hondas) because their lack of enthusiasm for Japan somehow felt directed at me. That I felt the most comfortable of us all confirmed for me a suspicion that I had had for quite some time, the suspicion that while I was an important part of the band, I was still quite different from the others in a way that mattered quite a bit. I know I didn't handle it well either, coming fully out as a person of color in the scene, my anger about the racism and the shame, unfocused and unexplained, sometimes directed at Adrienne, Karin, and Dominique when it shouldn't have been.

It was fitting that it was in Japan that Adrienne revealed to us that she was thinking of leaving the band. She told us in our room at Naoki's that she had been thinking about it for a while. I was not surprised, but while I was still unable to acknowledge the cancer of silence that had grown inside me, I was still crushed because while I had begun to find my identity outside of the band, my identity and sense of self was still very much connected to being in Spitboy. Maybe it hadn't just been Japan that had been difficult for Adrienne; maybe it was the pressure of being Adrienne from Spitboy, too, or maybe she wanted to make the move before we all grew apart even more.

Spitboy: The Creation Story

S he doesn't remember this, but Adrienne and I actually met in the fall of 1987, three years before we started Spitboy. I had spent the summer walking up and down Haight Street, making new city friends, but the City College semester had started, and I was already on my way to flunking out before it had really even gotten underway. Adrienne was going to City College too, taking classes with her boyfriend Doug, guitar player for Christ on Parade, a Bay Area political punk band. While on campus one day, Suzy and I introduced ourselves to them after she had recognized Doug after seeing Christ On Parade play at Gilman. We were still country girls who didn't understand city rules or that it might be weird to go up to someone at school to gush about how we saw their band play.

Doug was a punk icon and Adrienne looked so cool in her long black skirt, baggy top, and lace tied in her hair. I remember thinking it was cool that they were in school too, even though I knew I wouldn't be there for long since I didn't have any idea what I was doing, how the system worked, or if I really even belonged there. What I really wanted to be doing was playing music like Christ on Parade. It's why Suzy, Nicole, and I, Bitch Fight, had moved from Tuolumne to San Francisco. We knew going to school was a good idea, but it's not where our hearts were then; that came later.

My path would not cross Adrienne's again for another three years, and by then I felt like a completely different person, changing so much so quickly the way you do when you're eighteen, nineteen, and twenty. I was looking to start another band in which I'd play drums after Bitch Fight had broken up, but I was invited to join Kamala and Karnivores. They asked me to play guitar, which I was terrible at, but I needed the camaraderie, and for some reason they were really patient with me.

Adrienne and I were introduced anew by my then boyfriend, Neil, who would later learn to play bass and form his own band Paxston Quiggly. Neil had gotten to know Doug from Christ on Parade and had somehow gotten his hands on a tape that Doug and Adrienne had recorded, which he played for me. I loved Adrienne's voice right away, even though it's not the same voice that would later become associated with Spitboy, and I urged Neil to invite Doug and his girlfriend over to the warehouse where he lived at the time, so I could get to know her and find out if she was interested in starting a band.

We were sitting in the loft of Neil's warehouse when I told Adrienne about how we had met all those three years ago, which really felt like ten, as I had already been in two bands, lived in five different apartments, and dated three different scenesters: a stage hand, a drummer, and a record label guy. I liked Adrienne right away, yet she seemed so different than when I met her that faroff foggy day at City College. She laughed a natural hearty laugh when I told her about how Suzy and I had introduced ourselves to her and she had shook our hands and said nothing. It surprised me the way she spoke about herself.

"I was so insecure then." She laughed again shook her head. "I was a different person. I had gained a lot of weight and I didn't feel good about myself."

I had never really heard anyone speak so honestly about herself before. It was refreshing. Then she talked about creating her feminist punk zine *Too Far*. I had to convince her to be in my band. I introduced Paula to the hesitant Adrienne, who it turned out was looking to make some big changes in her life (like no longer being referred to as someone's girlfriend—to have a name and an identity all her own), and we talked her into starting the band with us. Paula knew Karin from Blacklist and heard that Harry and Lance from Cringer had taught her to play bar chords on guitar. Before long, we tested our compatibility, borrowing a practice room in East Oakland from some band we were friends with at the time. I was the only woman who had been in band or written songs, so I knew I had to come prepared with something to work on. It was a simple, three-chord song about a night two guys in a visiting punk band sexually harassed me at a party at my house.

The borrowed practice space, which smelled of sweat, beer, and cigarettes, hummed with palpable excitement and chemistry. Adrienne charmed everyone with her amazing openness, Karin wowed us with her crunchy guitar sound and bright smile, Paula grounded us with her generous spirit, and I brought experience and knowhow. We all knew of one another and already respected each other's work in the punk scene, and now we were in one room, exploring the possibility of being part of the scene together. My skeleton song, Karin's guitar sound, Adrienne's fierce vocals, and Paula's steady beat coalesced and took a shape all its own. By the end of that trial practice, there was no question; we were a band.

By the end of the second practice, we had secured a less temporary practice space, determined regular practice days and times, and had completed writing our first song, "Seriously," on which I was now singing backup vocals and playing drums, the song barely recognizable from the version I wrote on my acoustic guitar. The song was tough, and vulnerable, and it had attitude. It sounded like something totally fresh and new, like the female punk band I had been waiting to hear, waiting to discover for some time, the band that I was now in with Karin, and Paula, and Adrienne, the band that would soon be named after a female-body-centric creation story, a story that didn't involve god, a rib, or a man.

Spitboy and Roadie Phyllis (Tourettes), Reno, NV, U.S. tour 1994.

Acknowledgments

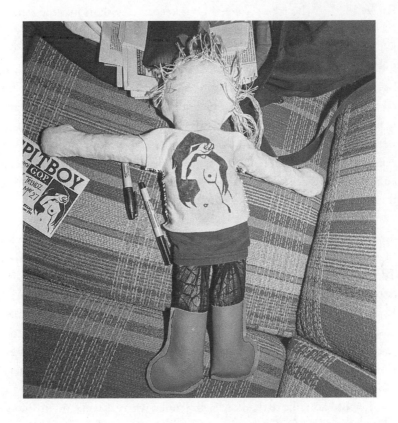

When I wrote the first piece of this collection, "The Spitboy Rule," I didn't know that I'd write a whole book or if people would even care until some really great people encouraged me to tell the story—people who saw the beauty in it before I did, people who saw the historical importance. Thank you Karin Spirn, Tomas Moniz, Heidi Avelina Smith, and mí media naranja, Inés Peralta.

And thank you to all the Wayward Writers who read early pieces, and who have cobbled together a writing community that includes mothers, their children, husbands, wives, dogs, and the first writing community that I have joined where I wasn't the only woman of color or the only Latina. Thank you to some of the most talented, kick-ass women that I've ever met: Ariel Gore, Margaret Garcia, Jenny Forrester, Lisbeth Coiman, Rebeca Dunn-Krahn, Jenny Hayes, Linda Cayot, and Rocky Hatley, who is not a woman but keeps up with us just the same.

I also have to thank Mimi Thi Nguyen and Martín Sorrondeguy for being such an important part of this project, for testifying for me, for Spitboy, and for helping to preserve the legacy. And thank you to the Spitboy photographers who submitted their work for this project, for taking so many great photos, for documenting the band so well in a time before digital cameras or widespread use of the internet. Thank you Lyn Lentil, Chris Boarts Larson, David Sine, Ace Morgan, John Lyons, and especially to Karoline Collins, who toured with the band, helped load equipment and sell merchandise, and took amazing photos (including the cover photo), capturing so much.

Many others deserved to be thanked, those who have supported me in a variety of ways since I began this project: Shawna Kenny, Jes Skolnik, Wendy-O Matik, Matt Wobensmith, Ann Imig and Listen To Your Mother; my Las Positas College family, especially the English department/Rawk Hawks, and Rafael Valle; Grace Ebron and Ann Romero at the Statewide Puente Office; Kirsten Saxton, Ajuan Mance, Gigi Pandian, Breezy Barcelo, Kendra Levine, Pat Libby, Naoki Ando, Jesse Townley, Matthew Thompson, Jesse Michaels, Nyky Gomez, Corbett Redford, Thang Nguyen, Nancy Davis Kho, Owen Peery, Martín Salazar, Jen Mahl, and Alice Bag.

I would also like to thank Melvin Jenner, we miss you, and my mom, Cheryl Gonzales, for having the courage to leave her abuser, my bio dad, and for teaching me to stand up for myself no matter what.

If I had an agent, I'd thank her too, but I do have PM Press, and they have been amazing. Thank you Romy and Ramsey for guiding me gently to write a better, fuller, more honest book, to John Yates for the beautiful cover design, and to Steven Stothard, Stephanie Pasvankias, Jonathan Rowland, and Gregory Nipper.

And finally, thank you Adrienne Stone, Paula Hibbs-Rines, Karin Gembus, and Dominique Davison. I hope I have captured our time together with all the honesty and affection it, and each of you, deserves.

Photo Credits

All photographs are courtesy of the author's personal collection unless noted otherwise.

Page 1: With Nicole Lopez circa 1985.

Page 6: 404 Willis, Detroit 1992. Photo: Ace Morgan.

Page 11: Spitboy graffiti.

Page 15: The author with Aaron Cometbus in Madison, WI, 1992. Photo: Karoline Collins.

Page 21: Woodcut by Jeff Hill.

Page 25: Spitboy at Olde West Studios with Kevin Army, circa 1992. Photo: John Lyons.

Page 28: With Trotsky and Spider, Citizen Fish and Amebix drummers, England, 1993.

Page 33: Spitboy Wall, New Zealand 1995. Photo: Ross Gardiner.

Page 39: Smash Sexism, New Zealand 1995. Photo: Ross Gardiner.

Page 44: Author with Chino Horde and friends, Little Rock, AR, 1992. Photo: Adrienne Stone.

Page 47: The author and her grandma, Delia Barraza.

Page 52: Spitboy with European tour road crew, Belgium, 1993.

Page 77: Spitboy with Ian MacKaye and Mark Andersen, Arlington, VA, 1994.

Page 81: Pete the Roadie, Forte Prenestino, Rome, Italy, 1992.

Page 86: Author at 924 Gilman, circa 1992. Photo: John Lyons.

Page 91: Spitboy in New Brunswick, NJ, 1994. Photo: Chris Boarts Larson.

Page 97: Spitboy Pies, Aotearoa, New Zealand. Photo: Lyn Spencer and Ross Gardiner.

Page 104: The author in Australia, 1995. Photo: Karoline Collins.

Page 108: Spitboy on arrival in Japan, 1995. Photo: Karoline Collins.

Page 115: José and Martín of Los Crudos, circa 1994.

Page 120: Karin and Michelle backstage, Japan, 1995. Photo: Karoline Collins.

Page 126: Spitboy in Kalamazoo, MI, 1992.

Michelle Cruz Gonzales was born in East LA in 1969 but grew up in Tuolumne, a tiny California Gold Rush town. She started her first band in that small town at the age of fifteen and moved to San Francisco two years later. She played drums and wrote lyrics for three bands during the 1980s and 1990s: Bitch Fight, Spitboy, and Instant Girl. In 2001 and 2003 she earned degrees in English/creative writing from Mills College, where she also minored in ethnic studies. Michelle has

Photo: Thang Nguyen

published in anthologies, literary journals, and *Hip Mama* magazine. She teaches English and creative writing at Las Positas College, and she enjoys reading her work and lecturing at colleges and art spaces around the country. She sings and plays drums in an English department band, loves to sew with her mom, even though she never thought she would, and she's at work on a satirical novel about forced intermarriage between whites and Mexicans for the purpose of creating a race of beautiful, hardworking people. She lives with her husband, son, and their three Mexican dogs in Oakland, California. You can find her at http://pretty-bold-mexican-girl.com or @xicanabrava.

About PM Press

PM Press was founded at the end of 2007 by a small collection of folks with decades of publishing, media, and organizing experience. PM Press co-conspirators have published and distributed hundreds of books, pamphlets, CDs, and DVDs. Members of PM have founded enduring book fairs, spearheaded victorious tenant organizing campaigns, and worked closely with bookstores, academic conferences, and even rock bands to deliver political and challenging ideas to all walks of life. We're old enough to know what we're doing and young enough to know what's at stake.

We seek to create radical and stimulating fiction and nonfiction books, pamphlets, T-shirts, visual and audio materials to entertain, educate, and inspire you. We aim to distribute these through every available channel with every available technology, whether that means you are seeing anarchist classics at our bookfair stalls; reading our latest vegan cookbook at the café; downloading geeky fiction e-books; or digging new music and timely videos from our website.

PM Press
PO Box 23912
Oakland, CA 94623
www.pmpress.org

Friends of PM Press

These are indisputably momentous times – the financial system is melting down globally and the Empire is stumbling. Now more than ever there is a vital need for radical ideas.

In the years since its founding—and on a mere shoestring—PM Press has risen to the formidable challenge of publishing and distributing knowledge and entertainment for the struggles ahead. With hundreds of releases to date, we have published an impressive and stimulating array of literature, art, music, politics, and culture. Using every available medium, we've succeeded in connecting those hungry for ideas and information to those putting them into practice.

Friends of PM allows you to directly help impact, amplify, and revitalize the discourse and actions of radical writers, filmmakers, and artists. It provides us with a stable foundation from which we can build upon our early successes and provides a much-needed subsidy for the materials that can't necessarily pay their own way. You can help make that happen—and receive every new title automatically delivered to your door once a month—by joining as a Friend of PM Press. And, we'll throw in a free T-Shirt when you sign up.

Here are your options:

+ $30 a month: Get all books and pamphlets plus 50% discount on all webstore purchases
+ $40 a month: Get all PM Press releases (including CDs and DVDs) plus 50% discount on all webstore purchases
+ $100 a month: Superstar—Everything plus PM merchandise, free downloads, and 50% discount on all webstore purchases

For those who can't afford $30 or more a month, we're introducing Sustainer Rates at $15, $10 and $5. Sustainers get a free PM Press t-shirt and a 50% discount on all purchases from our website.

Your Visa or Mastercard will be billed once a month, until you tell us to stop. Or until our efforts succeed in bringing the revolution around. Or the financial meltdown of Capital makes plastic redundant. Whichever comes first.

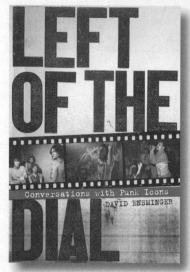
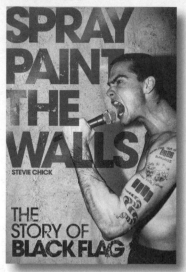
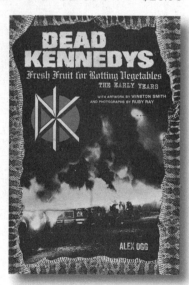
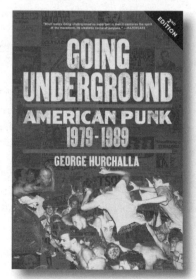